Alex.

MESSAGES FROM THE
MONEY MASTERS

Showcasing 12 Financial Experts'

Top Tips for Financial Success

To all you future $$ Successes !

BY JAY KEMMERER

[signature]

net worlding
PUBLISHING

MESSAGES FROM THE MONEY MASTERS

Showcasing 12 Financial Experts' Top Tips for Financial Success

BY JAY KEMMERER

Print: 978-1-944027-40-7

eBook: 978-1-944027-41-4

TABLE OF CONTENTS

INTRODUCTION: WHY THIS BOOK AND WHY NOW

I was raised in Oley, Pennsylvania, a small rural town near Reading by hard-working parents. My father worked two jobs for his entire life while supporting five kids. In other words, I was used to wearing hand-me-down clothes growing up. (I still remember getting my first pair of bell bottoms!)

My parents raised me to be a hard, honest worker. But early on in life, though I realized the significance of these values, I knew they were not enough to rely upon to get "rich." So in 1984, as a young man and aspiring investment professional, I embarked on a career in the wealth management industry. Then in 2008 and 2009, I decided to begin writing down everything I'd learned in my career.

My goal was to share my experiences to make a positive difference in peoples' financial lives and help those who had been impacted by The Great Recession. While my formal education proved invaluable, it was the information I gleaned from business seminars, books, from financially successful colleagues, my advisory team and even tips passed along on the golf course that seemed to have the most value. It was advice shared over dinner and in casual conversations with proven financial experts that gave me the "real world" wisdom I've applied in my practice. It's all about hearing the stories of clients and strangers whether told over drinks, in my office, on a plane, or at a conference that I remember most. When people feel safe, understood, or anonymous they are the most honest about the one thing we all are afraid to talk about—our money.

Over the years, throughout all these conversations, (and sometimes confessions) what I've learned is that people don't *plan* to make financial missteps. Rather, they simply don't invest the time and effort to educate themselves on financial matters. Unless you love numbers, it's boring or intimidating to stare at the kind of traditional financial advice you find online. Instead, most of us often choose to rely on friends or family members for advice, and those folks may or may not be experts on the subject of finance. Or, they hear a snippet of a television commercial, read a book, listen to a podcast, or talk among their friends as I did.

Unless their friends are financial experts too, they'll most likely create a financial soup of advice and practices from old wives' tales, inaccurate sources or outdated rules. Then, they'll follow it like it was sound financial advice when it's really just a collection of rabbits' feet (good luck), charms, and random luck. They've done essentially what we all do—look to others for advice—but their sources weren't or aren't filtered or vetted for accuracy. The one thing I know is not going to change is, we're not going to stop collecting and incorporating advice into our lives. It just makes sense to find, collect, and incorporate good, sound advice.

In this book, I will share the proven financial tips I've learned, tested, and have seen good results from implementing. This is the advice I give my clients to help them make the most of every financial opportunity in order to achieve, at a minimum, millionaire net worth status, financial independence, and financial success. I will also introduce simple financial principles from twelve experts many would call "the masters" in the financial wellness space. Together, the insights I will share should help you build a winning financial strategy, one that can help you develop a lifetime of financial achievements.

This book is not about getting rich quickly. Rather, it's about sharing the insights of the many experts – the wisdom of the crowd if you will, to help you become more financially savvy. Hopefully, you'll enjoy the stories and tips here and be motivated to pursue more financial education. If you can become more knowledgeable about basic economic principles, that knowledge will help you steer clear of the major financial mistakes so many people make. Regardless of the economic cycle or climate you're living in at this moment, there are financial opportunities that you can take advantage of *today*. Ultimately, the stories that I share throughout this book will help you learn, adopt, and practice the skills of creating, adhering to, and building your own powerful financial foundation.

There are millions of financial resources online and off for people of all income levels with any variety of assets and liabilities. You can contact your own CPA, or find one, or seek out a financial advisor who is willing to help guide you through the process of getting financially sound enough to begin investing. Everyone's needs and financial status are different. That's why I've included a chapter on assessing what you need, and what questions to ask any financial advisor before hiring them.

Many of those reading this book can find the additional information they need online, or by reading any of the books, articles, or resources listed at the end. Dave Ramsey's Financial Peace University has changed hundreds of thousands of lives for the better. His "debt snowball" concept has helped millions of people become debt-free, and the process is described free on his website, and in this book.

Something many of us don't know is that significant numbers of people move into poverty throughout their lives. In fact, slightly more than half (51.4%) of the U.S. population experiences poverty at some time before age 65. The chance of becoming poor is roughly 4% a year, but this figure does not reflect the number who cycle through poverty over the course of their lives. People are more likely to experience poverty at younger ages. About 35% of people are poor between ages 20 and 40, compared with 23% between age 40 and 60. Also, household heads under age 25 are significantly more likely to become poor.[1] I like how TED Global speaker and formerly homeless author Becky Blanton describes poverty and homelessness—"It's a place WHERE you are. It's not WHO you are." Others have been where you are and moved on and up and you can also.

Most of the financial masters listed here didn't start off rich, or even financially comfortable. Suze Orman lived in a van and waited tables for seven years. Tony Robbins was a janitor from a broken family. Daymond John was living with his mother and working at Red Lobster. Dave Ramsey amassed a $4 million real estate portfolio by the time he was 26 years old, only to lose it by the time he was 30. He owed millions and went bankrupt before figuring out how to manage money. After becoming a millionaire twice, Mike Michalowicz lost every dollar he owned because of poor investments he made.

I do not call them Financial Experts because they never made a mistake and have always been wealthy. I call them Financial Experts because they emerged from poverty to become wealthy. And the things they learned along the way have proven to be wisdom all of us can learn from. Don't think you have to be a genius, gifted, or love numbers to follow their advice. Daymond John and others admit they don't love numbers and aren't good with them, and yet still became millionaires. When you start making, saving and investing your money, you can hire people who love numbers!

These masters have seen success in their own lives, books and podcasts. Their advice has helped their readers and followers succeed as well. How you learn and implement advice best is up to you. I know if you're

---

[1] https://www.urban.org/sites/default/files/publication/30636/411956-Transitioning-In-and-Out-of-Poverty.PDF

dedicated and serious about managing your money and becoming finan-cially savvy, you can do it. Discipline, education, and commitment mean more than book or money smarts. Money management may sound intimidating, but basic money management is not rocket science. I hope the stories and examples in this book prove that. You're not alone. I have helped people with $30,000 a year or below incomes as well as multi-millionaires navigate the basics of budgets, saving, investments, and money discipline. I can help you, too, if you're willing to do the work. Now, let's meet the masters:

MEET THE MASTERS

To become an expert in financial matters—whether it's your personal finances or your business finances, it's critical to study the habits and beliefs of successful financial gurus; those men and women who have actually put their ideas into action and successfully implemented them over and over again. While I can't compile their entire financial history here, I can pull out their best tips and processes. Here are a few experts that we'll be talking about in the book who will inspire you on your financial journey. I've listed them in alphabetical order by their last names, not in order of any particular preference:

DAVID BACH

As one of America's most trusted, legendary personal finance experts and bestselling financial authors, David Bach has 12 national bestsellers to his credit. He is also a motivational speaker, entrepreneur, television personality, podcaster and the founder of FinishRich.com.

One of David's insightful pieces of advice is, "Once your values are clear your financial decisions become easy." Born in 1966 in Oakland, California, David went on to attend USC. Following graduation, he be-gan working as a financial advisor. A number of his clients were self-made millionaires, despite earning average salaries. Always a quick study, by heeding their advice David soon learned and further developed his "pay-yourself-first" methodology that has become a mainstay in his writing and consulting.

In 2019, he cowrote *The Latte Factor: Why You Don't Have to Be Rich to Live Rich* with John David Mann. In this relatable parable, they teach readers three secrets to financial freedom. The protagonist, Zoey, is a young professional working and living in New York City. As with many people in their 20s, Zoey struggles to make financial ends meet, but through tiny changes she makes every day, she gains a wealth of knowledge about how to be smarter about money and those insights are compellingly shared with the reader. His website, like his advice, is straightforward – www.davidbach.com

RONALD S. BARON

Ronald S. Baron (aka Ron Baron) is a billionaire American mutual fund manager and investor, and the founder of Baron Capital, a New York-based investment management firm. He founded Baron Funds in 1982 and is its CEO. It's a money management firm with $30 billion in assets under management as of September 2019. Baron Growth, the buy-and-hold investor's $7 billion flagship fund, has an annual turnover of just 3%. He was born in Asbury Park, New Jersey in 1943, to Morton and Marian Baron. His parents both were government employees; Morton was a Fort Monmouth engineer, and Marian was a purchasing agent at Camp Evans.

Ron has shared other insights into his childhood, such as the fact that for a time, his family lived in a 3-room garage apartment that was so small there was no room for a refrigerator. So they kept that appliance on the porch.

Showing a keen interest in earning money from a young age, Ron's industrious first odd jobs included waiting tables, working as a lifeguard, shoveling snow, being a golf caddy and more. When he earned his first

$1,000 from all of these endeavors along with some Bar Mitzvah gifts, he talked his dad into letting him make his first investment at the age of 14. He checked the stock reports every day after school, and by the time he entered college, he had parlayed it into $4,000. That earned him the nickname of "Count" among his friends, and that has stuck to this day.

Ron studied chemistry at Bucknell University and received a scholarship to George Washington University Law School, which he attended at night. He worked for a number of brokerage firms from 1970 until 1982 and earned a reputation as an astute investor in small companies.

Fortune magazine dubbed him, "the Warren Buffett of small and mid-cap stocks," and Forbes magazine lists him in the top 400 wealthiest Americans. You can learn more about him on his company website - www.baronfunds.com

WARREN BUFFETT

Warren Buffett, the CEO of Berkshire Hathaway, is the third richest person in the world with a net worth of over $85 billion. However, he's regarded by most as the number one stock-picker in the world. He's earned a couple of well-deserved nicknames for his gift: "The Oracle of Omaha" and "The Sage of Omaha." He is also known as a business magnate, investor, speaker, and philanthropist. Born in Nebraska in 1930, he showed an amazing acumen for business at a young age. His father Howard was a stockbroker and U.S. Congressman.

Warren graduated from the University of Nebraska with a Bachelor of Science in Business Administration when he was just 19 years old. He was rejected by Harvard Business School but went on to obtain a Master of Science in Economics from Columbia University in 1951. He then attended the New York Institute of Finance.

In 1956, he formed Buffett Partnership Ltd. He had an innate knack for identifying companies that were undervalued and invested wisely. This is the skill that made him a millionaire. In 1965 at the age of 35, he took the reins at Berkshire Hathaway, a textile company in which he had purchased several shares of stock. He phased out the textile manufacturing capacity and steered the corporation into the purchase of media assets such as *The Washington Post*. He pioneered Berkshire Hathaway's substantial investment in Coca-Cola and became director of it from 1989 until 2006.

A billionaire many times over, Buffett is one of the richest men in the world and is also an amazingly generous philanthropist. In 2006 he announced he was giving away his entire fortune, having pledged 85% of it to the Bill and Melinda Gates Foundation, which became the largest charitable giving act in the history of the U.S. In 2010, Buffett and Gates co-created The Giving Pledge Campaign, through which they encourage and mentor wealthy benefactors to donate to philanthropic causes.

When he received a diagnosis of prostate cancer in 2012, he successfully completed treatment and is still going strong. There are many great books about Buffett's career and life. Along with Charlie Munger, in my estimation, Warren Buffett is a phenomenal stock-picker. His philosophy is this: You buy a good company and you hold that company for a long, long time. He's not a market timer. He doesn't try to pick the hot stock of the day, the week or the year.

When the technology boom was initially happening back in 1998-2000, right before the NASDAQ bust where it lost 85% of its value, Warren Buffett's take on that was, "I don't understand these technology companies, so I can't invest in them." If you look at what he has traditionally committed assets to, he's invested in recession-proof type industries like insurance, food, beverage and banks.

He believes in concentrating your holdings. He doesn't believe that you need 200 companies, like most mutual funds. He believes in focusing on 20 or fewer companies in a portfolio. One of Buffett's quotes sums up this philosophy: "When we own portions of outstanding businesses with outstanding managements, our favorite holding period is forever."

His three most famous sayings are:

- "Rule No. 1: Never lose money. Rule No. 2: Never forget rule No. 1."
- "If the business does well, the stock eventually follows."
- "It's far better to buy a wonderful company at a fair price than a fair company at a wonderful price."

His website is www.berkshirehathaway.com

HARRY DENT

Harry was born in 1953 in Columbia, South Carolina. His father, Harry S. Dent, Sr. was an American politician and political strategist. Harry, Jr. studied economics in college during the 1970s, but found his course-work too vague and inconclusive for his taste. That's when he embarked upon his career as a finance writer who identified and delved into the fields of demographics, technology, consumer finance and multiple trends in the financial area that helped him cultivate the ability to fore-cast economic shifts. Harry received his MBA from Harvard Business School. His website is easy to remember – www.harrydent.com

He is a prolific writer, with several bestsellers to his credit. During his career, Dent has worked globally with executives, investors and finan-cial advisors. A veteran of television appearances, he's been on *Good Morning America*, as well as CNBC, CNN/Fox News and PBS. Prestig-ious publications such *as Barron's, Fortune, Success, U.S. News and World Report* and many others have featured his writing.

I met Harry Dent in Boston in the early '90s. He had just written a book called *The Great Boom Ahead*. If you go back in time and read that book, he was 100% right on the money. He made this comment in a meeting in '91: "It doesn't matter who the next president of the United States will be. They're going to be enjoying the credit for one of the greatest financial booms that this country has ever seen."

He's a notable demographic analyst. He astutely stated that based on the wave and the ages of those baby boomers back then, he accurately predicted what areas of the economy were really going to do well and what areas within the country were going to do well. He was proficient in assessing the future baby boomers spending habits and desire to upgrade into larger homes. Economic conditions may always play a major role in most financial decisions.

LORI GREINER

Lori is known as an investor on the reality TV show *Shark Tank* and on its spin-off, *Beyond the Tank*. In 2000, before becoming a regular on *Shark Tank* in 2012, Lori was best known as the "Queen of QVC" along with her show *Clever & Unique Creations*. Greiner is the president and founder of the company, For Your Ease Only, Inc. and is the author of *Invent it, Sell it, Bank it! – Make Your Million Dollar Idea into a Reality*, a how-to guide based on her entrepreneurial journey. Lori holds the honor of having one of the biggest successes in *Shark Tank* history. No one had any idea her 2014 investment in Scrub Daddy, a company that produces a texture-changing household sponge, would do as well as it did.

An inventor herself, in 1997, Greiner created and patented a plastic earring organizer. JCPenney picked up the organizer before the holiday season and resulting sales paid off the $300,000 loan she took out to produce it in only eighteen months. Greiner tells readers, "When I created my first product, all I had was a great idea and a tireless work ethic—and no clue where to start. So I taught myself everything there is to know about taking an idea and turning it into millions."

Millions is right. According to a variety of sources, including *Shark Tank*, Greiner's net worth is $50 million dollars. While she began her business career by designing a jewelry box that had the capacity to hold 100 pairs of earrings, she's not a "one-trick pony." She generated $1 million in revenue in the first year of selling her jewelry box, then moved on to invent, market and sell other products before joining *Shark Tank* in 2012.

DAYMOND JOHN

John Garfeld Daymond, or Daymond John, is best known for his presence as an investor on the ABC reality television series *Shark Tank*. A multitasking tour de force, John is an American businessman, investor, television personality, author, and motivational speaker, best known as the founder, president, and CEO of FUBU. FUBU is an American hip-hop apparel company. FUBU is the acronym for "For Us, By Us." Based in New York City, John is the founder of The Shark Group.

His bestselling book, *The Power of Broke*, is just one in a series of books he has written about money and wealth. *Rise and Grind, Power Shift*, and *The Brand Within* are all books that give readers tips on money and investing, but more importantly on attitude and self.

ROBERT KIYOSAKI

A Japanese American who was born in Hilo, Hawaii, Kiyosaki made his fortunes after a lifetime of struggles, bankruptcies and failures, reaching success only after he was almost 50 years old.

His *Rich Dad, Poor Dad* book series begins with a comparison between his two 'dads': one his poor biological father, the other a fictitious rich dad. It is an international bestseller. The poor father was in fact very educated but had no money; the rich father was a high school dropout but was in fact 'Hawaii's richest man.' He uses examples in the book to show readers how they can succeed regardless of age or background if they follow the principles of the 'rich dad.'

Kiyosaki draws on his own life experiences in the book. After graduating from high school, he went to the U.S Merchant Marine Academy and graduated as a deck officer in 1969. He went on to serve in Vietnam and was honored with the Air Medal after serving as a gunship pilot. Six years later he left the Marine Corps and became a Xerox machine sales-person. Three years after that he launched his own company that sold Velcro surfer wallets. While the company did well for some time, it eventually went bankrupt. He would be no stranger to bankruptcy or financial failure over his life.

Undeterred by the wallet failure, he moved on to a business selling cer-tified heavy metal rock band T-shirts. He sold the T-shirt business in 1985 but continued to struggle for nearly a decade more. His fortunes changed in 1997 when he established Cashflow Technologies, Inc., which incorporates and runs two of his brands, namely Rich Dad and Cashflow.

NAPOLEON HILL

Often thought of as the father of prosperity consciousness and manifes-tation, Hill's flagship book *Think and Grow Rich* first appeared in 1937. The initial P.R. touted it as a "personal development and self-improve-ment book." While that's true, it is so much more. It was a landmark book due to the fact that it was one of the first times that an American author wrote about the concept of Mastermind group power as well as what became and still is still a big buzz phrase – The Law of Attraction. In other words, whatever you focus your thoughts and energy upon be-come your reality (i.e., "thoughts are things.")

Hill went on to write several other books, among them *Own Your Own Mind, The Law of Success: In Sixteen Lessons*, and *Outwitting the Devil: The Secret to Freedom and Success*. In modern society, a number of questionable actions from his history prior to his own immense success have cast some aspersions upon Hill's personal integrity. For one thing, it is undocumented that he ever actually met steel magnate and self-made millionaire Andrew Carnegie, from whom he claimed to learn about Mastermind principles. Yet it is undeniable that Hill's eventual success and the high esteem in which many still hold him today proves that he shared valuable groundbreaking information on how to attract wealth.

Think and Grow Rich has been the inspiration for the concepts behind the book and movie *The Secret*. Many of the other financial gurus I've listed in this biography section have given him credit for their inspiration.

You can research the controversial information about Hill if you wish; it's there for your consideration. Ultimately, though, his writing and legacy about money and how to attract and manage it have basically far exceeded any bad rap attributed to him. If you'd like to learn more about the man, his philosophy and events based on his teaching, visit www.naphill.org

MIKE MICHALOWICZ

Early in his career, Mike Michalowicz was a small business columnist for *The Wall Street Journal*. He was the "Business Rescue" segment host for MSNBC's *Your Business* and he hosted the reality television program called *Bailout!* A former monthly columnist for *The Wall Street Journal's* small-business section, Mike also wrote the WSJ's Small Business Shortcuts series. He is a contributor to *Entrepreneur Magazine* and is a columnist for American Express's "Open Forum" series.

He's made over ten appearances on CNBC's The Big Idea with Donny Deutsch and has also appeared on NBC, MSNBC, Fox News, ABC News Now, CNBC's On the Money and Pat Croce's Down To Business. He currently speaks and lectures at universities, corporations, and organizations around the world on entrepreneurship, sales, and behavioral marketing techniques.

He's also the author of five books about business, money, and entrepreneurship including, *Profit First*, a book about paying yourself first.

Mike is the co-founder and CEO of Profit First Professionals, a membership organization for accountants, bookkeepers, and consultants who use the book *Profit First* to guide businesses to higher and consistent levels of profitability. Profit First Professionals has members from over ten countries, including the United States, Canada, Mexico, Australia, England, Germany, and the Netherlands.

In Mike's first book, *The Toilet Paper Entrepreneur*, he describes entrepreneurship like being in a bathroom with only three sheets of toilet paper left on the roll. "Somehow," he writes, "with the help of the trashcan remnants, you still manage to make it work." That, he explains, is how a Toilet Paper Entrepreneur runs their business... they make do with what they have, pull "miracles" out of the trash and make more and more with less and less.

Mike's road to fame and fortune hasn't always been easy. He founded and sold two multimillion-dollar companies by the age of 35, but then literally lost everything he owned after making poor decisions as an angel investor. In his books and on his podcasts he talks about learning he'd lost everything, and how his 9-year daughter left the room only to return with her piggy-bank, offering to give him all her money to help.

He didn't need her savings, just a little time. In the following years, he wrote five books and climbed back to the top, where he's now working on his third million-dollar business.

SUZE ORMAN

Suze Orman wears a number of hats, and wears them all very well, including bestselling author, financial advisor, television and podcast host, and motivational speaker. She is a six-time Emmy winner and authored six consecutive New York Times bestsellers. She hails from Chicago and was born there in 1951.

She spent seventeen years a stockbroker at Merrill Lynch, Prudential Bache and was the head of her own firm before appearing on Oprah, and eventually morphing into a household name as a global personal finance expert.

In one of her early books, *The 9 Steps to Financial Freedom: Practical and Spiritual Steps So You Can Stop Worrying*, she frankly shared some of her personal history. She was working as a waitress in a small town, barely clearing $10,000 annually. Some of her regular customers were stockbrokers and they realized she had an amazing personality and was incredibly bright. One of them recommended she apply to become a stockbroker at Merrill Lynch.

Even though she had her doubts about this major career change, she bolstered up her courage and went through with it. Merrill Lynch hired her in 1980 as a financial advisor, and within three short years, she moved to Prudential Securities, accepting the title of vice president of retail customer investments. In 1987, she founded the Suze Orman Financial Group, and her television show went on the air in 2002.

In 2015 when *The Suze Orman Show* wrapped up its successful 13-year run, she and her wife Kathy Travis retired to the Bahamas, where they happily spend much of their time fishing on their small boat (compared to their neighbors' yachts). True, they have a beautiful mansion there, but are living the good life peacefully and far away from the public eye – most of the time. Suze still presents seminars and offers a wide array of financial tools in addition to her books. Check out her website for more details – www.suzeorman.com

DAVE RAMSEY

An American radio show host, businessman, and author, Dave Ramsey was born in Antioch, near Nashville, Tennessee in 1960. He obtained a Bachelor of Science degree in finance and real estate from the University of Tennessee. By the time he hit 26 years of age, Dave had amassed a $4 million real estate portfolio, only to lose it by the time he was 30.

Using the wisdom he gained from that experience, he reinvented his financial life. Since then he has been teaching others how to do the same by making smart, responsible decisions with their money so that they have enough to take care of loved ones, retire comfortably, and be able to donate generously to others. Dave's website is www.daveramsey.com

TONY ROBBINS

Since he is an extremely well-known author, motivational speaker, life coach, business strategist and philanthropist, many people are familiar with Tony Robbins' lifework as well as his personal "rags to riches" background. In case you're not all that well acquainted with that history, I'll share a bit of it with you here.

Born in 1960 in Glendora, California, Anthony Robbins grew up in a working-class family. At a young age, Tony began reading the works of Ralph Waldo Emerson and Dale Carnegie. When he was about 17 years old, Tony's mother kicked his father out of the house, and believing her son to be on his father's "side," she soon gave Tony the boot as well. His father had moved to the East Coast, so Tony had no place to live. He did have a job, though, and despite working long shifts, he was too broke to afford a place of his own. So he slept in the back of his car, with a coat for a blanket.

It was around this turbulent time in his young life that Tony had the epiphany that "The Secret to Living is Giving." He wrote that in his journal and made a conscious choice to focus on what he did want, rather than becoming bitter and focusing on what he did not have. Instead of attending college, he went to work for Jim Rohn, a motivational speaker. To this day he refers to Rohn as his first mentor.

Tony soon discovered he had a talent of his own for public speaking as well as for writing. He learned about neuro-linguistic programming (NLP) and began using it to improve his life. To date, he has written six bestselling books and given sold-out seminars around the globe. He is involved in a number of charities, including Feeding America and a water company called Spring Health, which brings clean water to eastern India, where the number one killer of children is waterborne diseases.

A number of famous people have gone through Tony's training and hold him in the highest esteem, actor Gerard Butler among them. Butler has said, "Fear is a huge issue for me. This technique Tony has is a really smart way to literally set those fears aside…That to me is unleashing the power within."

CHAPTER ONE
THE RICHER OR POORER QUESTION
— WHAT ARE YOUR FINANCIAL GOALS?

When John Pool went into a local convenience store to buy a soda a few years ago, he happened to notice the Missouri Powerball Jackpot had climbed to $40 million dollars.

"What the heck?" he thought. "I could use $40 million and if I don't win, it's only a buck." He dug in his pocket, pulled out a dollar bill and bought a lottery ticket. Even though John didn't win the $40 million dollar Powerball, he did win $50,000—not exactly chump change. When he went to claim his winnings, he told lottery officials that it was a "spur of the moment" decision to buy the ticket. He explained that he didn't think that he would actually win, but reminded officials like the saying goes, "You have to be in it to win it."[2]

Years ago Ryan Seiler of North Plainfield told New Jersey Lottery officials his decision to buy a few Powerball tickets when the jackpot reached $260 million was a spur of the moment decision. He bought his tickets only minutes before the lottery registers closed for the night. Seiler matched five of the six balls needed and won one million dollars as a result of his last-minute, impulsive decision.[3]

---

[2] https://www.playusalotteries.com/en/lottery-news/article/11719/last-minute-decision-pays-off-as-powerball-lottery-player-wins-50000-.html
[3] https://www.upi.com/Odd_News/2019/02/21/Man-buys-1-million-lottery-ticket-at-the-last-minute/8061550774584/

True, most of us will never win anything on *our* impulsive lottery ticket purchase. It's just an impulse buy, but then again… we might win or finesse our way out of poverty without having to think or do much about it.

So what does the lottery have in common with investing, or money, or financial management? Throwing down a dollar or two on the spur of the moment doesn't exactly equate with investing thousands, or hundreds of thousands of dollars in the stock market, or on real estate on a hunch, or in a "What the heck?" moment—or does it? For many of us, I think it does. We hope we're making good decisions. We're willing to risk our financial future on luck, guesses, and flying by the seat of our pants.

That alone is proof that money is more than just "money." It's a psychological gateway. How we earn it, save it, abuse it, ignore it, fear it, love it, hate it, spend it, or invest it tells us more about ourselves than we realize. There are thousands of books out there that can explain the basics of money to you. I even list a few dozen of my favorites at the end of this book. What I'm offering that others aren't are the emotional and psychological insights, tips, and stories about money that my clients, friends, strangers, and experts have to share, as well as practical advice.

Growing up, most of us get "the talk" about how to succeed, or how to understand aspects of life we haven't yet encountered. Whether it's 'the talk' about sex, or school, or life, or work or a career, people have a lot of advice to share. Unfortunately, not many of us get the "money talk." Most people I know would prefer talking about anything but their money—especially if they aren't managing it well. I know for a fact that I can teach you the basics of money: how to save, budget, and invest it, and you'll still struggle. People need more. They need to think about what money is, what it means to them, how they relate (or not) to it, and why, as one expert says, they "go to school to learn how to earn it, but never how to manage it."

So, before I launch into the basics, the tips, and the stories, relax for a minute. Let's start off with one basic question, something I like to call the "richer or poorer" question.

The Richer or Poorer Question

Smart investors and good money managers always ask themselves this question:

"Will I be richer or poorer tomorrow if I make this financial commitment today?"

John Pool and Ryan Seiler asked it when they were buying their lottery tickets. Okay, maybe it was less structured, something like, "Maybe I'll win, maybe not." But they considered, however roughly, how their decision to spend a dollar or two might impact their future.

"Will I be richer or poorer tomorrow if I make this financial commitment today?" It's a simple question, and oftentimes the answer is obvious, but other times it's not. The secret of asking this question is, if you listen to your answers they can tell you what your goals are, or if you really have no specific financial or life goals.

Ask yourself, "Will I be richer or poorer if I _____?"

- Buy a Mercedes (or other expensive new car)
- Go to Graduate School or back to college
- Sell my business
- Start a business
- Open a savings account
- Start an IRA or a 401K
- Get serious about learning how-to manage my money
- Leave my job and travel the world for a year
- Get married

- Have kids
- Get divorced
- Buy a condo
- Give up golf, or take up golf
- Eat more (or less) fast food
- Drop $50 on dinner and drinks
- Stop smoking
- Pack my lunch
- Make coffee at work rather than buy coffee on the way to work

Do you see where this is going? The fact is, every decision we make, or don't make, no matter how large or how small, ultimately makes us richer or poorer. It's not just the big decisions, like a new car, a new house, or a change in jobs. Our decision about where every dollar we make ultimately goes—even the cost of a cup of coffee, or bus fare versus walking or taking an Uber or Lyft is what makes us richer or poorer.

Suze Orman says she never pays for coffee because she can invest that $300 (two cups a day) a month into an interest earning account and have $250,000 saved in 40 years.

Dave Ramsey says never buy a brand-new car until you're 100% debt free and have a net worth of one million dollars. Who's right and who's wrong? They all are. That's the point. Stop seeing money as black or white, right or wrong. Money is a tool, and like any tool the thing that matters most is who is using it, and how they're using it. A craftsman can use nothing more than a few hand tools and create masterpiece and heirloom quality furniture. An unskilled newbie can own every tool ever invented and screw up making a simple box. Did you know many of the Pulitzer Award winning photographs from WWII were taken with a simple Brownie camera? In fact, Virginia Schau, the first woman to win a Pulitzer for photography, was a housewife using a Brownie camera with only two frames of photos on year-old film on it.[4] It's not the tools, it's what you can do with what you have.

That's how most of the financial experts I reference in this book were able to go from broke to billions. It's not the tools, their income, or the lucky breaks. It's them—their mindset, their persistence, courage, and decisions that made them richer, or at times poorer. The same is true for you. There's nothing exclusive about these experts. They came up from humble (poor) beginnings and learned and failed and got back up and tried again. None of them knew all the answers when they started. They learned, just like you're doing now, through trial and error. That's why I start my clients off with that one question whenever they're getting ready to spend anything. It can be very annoying to ask yourself, "Will I be richer or poorer if I buy this coffee?"

But when you get into the habit of consciously asking yourself that question, it eventually becomes a part of your routine, and then part of your financial discipline. You start seeing every purchase, no matter how small, in terms of your goals. Then, when you're considering the big purchases, you really see the power of asking.

A client of mine told me about encouraging his young children at the time, a son 6, and a daughter 8, to ask themselves this question years ago. They struggled with the concept of "richer or poorer," so he helped them set goals for their money. They both wanted bicycles. So whenever they were in the store and saw something to spend their allowance on, it was okay if they wanted to spend their money. However, he made them say out loud, "Will buying this ____ (toy or treat) help me get my bicycle sooner? That they understood. Sometimes they bought the treat or toy anyway, but eventually they realized delayed gratification has its advantages. By the time they were old enough to drive, both had saved enough money to buy the (used) cars they wanted. They then began to use their income to pay their portion of their car insurance. I know many

---

[4] https://birdinflight.com/inspiration/experience/20170623-pulitzer-by-chance.html

adults who can't do this. They've never learned how to set goals, delay gratification, or create a spending strategy.

Obviously making any financial commitment is simple if you have a goal and a strategy. Buying a Porsche because you want it doesn't seem very smart. But it can be a smart investment if you also happen to sell products and services to Porsche owners. While you don't have to have a Porsche to sell to Porsche owners, owning one would give you an unusual showroom with which to display your wares. You don't need it (think Brownie camera), but having a strategy for buying a Porsche makes more sense than just buying a Porsche because "It's cool and I want one."

Weighing your reasons, and potential outcomes when asking whether you'll be richer or poorer, or closer to purchasing something you want (your goal) is critical. Don't just talk yourself into buying it with clever arguments. Be realistic. When you ask yourself this question it can help direct your actions and thoughts in other ways.

When Richard, a friend of mine, decided to buy a three-bedroom condominium in a college town a few years ago, I was surprised. Given the state of the housing market, I didn't think it was a smart investment at the time. It didn't fit with any financial goals of his that I was aware of. Then he explained to me that he had three children, 12, 15, and 17, all of whom planned to attend the same college, his alma mater. He was looking at the cost of dorm and rental housing and food over four years and possibly 2-3 extra years of graduate school for each of them.

"I asked myself, 'Do I really want to pay $10,000 a year for dorm housing for 12 years?' The answer was no. Paying rent would just be pouring money down the drain," he told me. "I could pay $10,000 to $30,000 a year depending on which kids were in school, or I could invest that into a $100,000 condo. It made more sense to invest in the condo."

Buying the condo and making mortgage payments on it, then selling it when his children had all graduated and moved out, or renting it to other students suddenly made sense. At the very least he'd break even. At best he'd make a profit. The investment furthered his goal of investing in the kind of real estate that would ultimately bring him a healthy return. He took out a 15-year mortgage, as Dave Ramsey suggests in his program:

"Some people get a 30-year mortgage, thinking they'll pay it off in 15 years. Good intentions aside, this rarely happens. Why? Because life happens instead. You might decide to keep that extra payment and take a vacation. Or maybe it's time to upgrade your kitchen. What about a new wardrobe? Whatever it is, there's always a reason to spend that money somewhere else," Ramsey explains.

Monthly payments on a 15-year mortgage are higher from the beginning. There's a built-in accountability to get your house paid off fast because the payments are so high. Sure, a 30-year mortgage has a longer term, but your monthly payments will be lower even though your interest paid on the loan will be higher. That means you'll pay less money every month, but you'll also make payments for twice as long. Your bank will love you because they'll get thousands of dollars more in interest.

Richard showed me how he figured he'd be able to pay the mortgage off by the time all his kids had graduated. He'd make back the cost of his mortgage on the condo over the cost of 12-15 years of paying for a dorm room for each child. He'd read about this trend online. It sounded too obviously good to be true. So, he took the time to crunch the numbers to make sure he would 'richer' with the investment. He learned the money he'd have paid on a dorm room for one child each semester would almost cover the mortgage payments. When two kids were in school he'd cover the entire mortgage with what he was paying. In addition to the mortgage, his kids would have more living space, and they'd get to learn about cooking, shopping, and paying the other bills associated with independent living.

His children's roommates would pay the equivalent of the mortgage for the privilege of occupying the other two bedrooms. Their cost for rent was cheaper than the room and amenities than the dorm offered, so they and their parents were happy to pay it. He was relieved he had the foresight to seize the opportunity when it was offered, even though his realtor told him it was "overpriced for the area." But he saw the potential, asked the all-important question about 'richer or poorer,' and moved on it.

Sometimes "conventional wisdom" isn't the best thing to trust when making an investment. As Richard learned when you zig while others are zagging, you can make money instead of spending it. You have to be willing to look at things differently, to see and believe in a "less traveled way." When Richard invested in the condo he was doing so for a different reason than most real estate investors. When he asked himself whether his purchase would make him richer or poorer, he realized his end game wasn't to make a killing on a real estate deal, it was to save money on housing for his college aged kids. The criteria for his investment was different in this instance and he recognized that and acted. He paid more for the condo than a sound real estate investment might have cost, but he saved money on housing and tapped into what turned into a very good investment over time. He simply saw a different potential.

A client's friend of theirs, Rebecca, was moving from Denver, Colorado to Tennessee for a new job. She sold all but a van load's worth of things to move with her. The things she got rid of would just be cheaper to replace than move, the things she kept would be more expensive to replace. She checked all the prices for rental trucks and vans and was feeling pretty discouraged.

"With the cost of insurance, and needing a van, the cheapest rentals I could find at the time were still $800 and up for the rental and insurance for the week, and I'd still have to spend $400 to $500 on gas and food, so it would cost me at least $1,200," she explained. She thought about her options for a few days.

"I had to go back and forth with that question, 'Will keeping this stuff and renting a van make me richer or poorer?'" Next she got the idea to buy a used van she saw on Craigslist for $700, already $100 less than what the rental would cost. She figured she'd load it up and drive all her stuff back, and then resell the van and get most of her money back. She could get an out-of-state car transport tag for $10, and insure the van for transport under her current insurance carrier for $53 for the entire trip rather than the $25 a day the rental van insurance would cost her. She sold her car for $2,000, and used that money to buy the van, and then set the rest aside for gas and expenses for the trip.

The van was old. It looked like a paint store had exploded on it, but it ran well. She didn't need it to be pretty, she told me. She just needed it to run and get her and her stuff across the country. She loaded it up, barely getting everything she now owned, plus her and her dog into it. Then she drove it cross country for 3,500 odd miles, and sold it the following week for $600 ($100 less than she paid for it.) The entire move ended up costing her a little under $500 once she paid for insurance, transport tags, gas for the trip, and had an oil change and topped up the van's fluids to ensure it made the trip. She slept in the van, saving hotel expenses, and kept her food expenses down by eating at fast food places and making sandwiches along the way. It was extreme, but she was willing to do it for just a week to save money. If she had rented a van she says she figured the trip would have cost $1,300—$800 for the rental and insurance, and another $500 for gas and food.

"Even if I had had to sell it for parts at the end, I'd have spent much less than renting a newer van. It didn't have to look pretty or be comfortable. It just had to run for a week."

Yes, things could have gone wrong. The van could have broken down, and she might have had to rent a van after all, and still sell the van for scrap or parts, but it didn't break down. That was the risk she was willing to take and it paid off. The naysayers to her plan shut up, and she was glad she hadn't listened to them. She's not the only person who's had to buck their friend's advice.

"'Your product sucks!' You know how many times I've heard that in my career?" Daymond John recently asked his followers.

"If you are an entrepreneur, then I am sure you have heard this more times than you would like to. Let me guess, everyone is also telling you your product is stupid and isn't worth your time...

"I know this because I bet you are a lot like me and every successful entrepreneur will hear this at some point. Listen, those people are haters and are just jealous that you are five steps ahead of them," he said.

If the financial gurus and businessmen and women are hearing those kinds of negative responses from their friends, family, and strangers, you can bet your friends and family are going to say the same to you. Just understand that it's not you, it's them. In some weird way they think they're protecting and helping you by being negative. They're afraid and wouldn't make that same decision, so they try to stop you from making it.

Trust your gut, follow your instincts and do what you think is best for you. If you make mistakes, or I should say when you make mistakes (you will) learn from them and move on. Setbacks are normally temporary, and in the words of Joel Osteen," Setbacks are merely a setup for something greater ahead."

WHERE ARE YOU NOW?

Have you just graduated from school, started your first business or job, just gotten married, bought your first home, had your first child, or started planning for retirement? Have you recently retired, or just lost a parent or a loved one? No matter what your age or situation, life is happening to you right now. It always will. We are all continuously bombarded with life events that can either derail our dreams and aspirations or force us to reassess our financial situation. You're not alone. Every-one, at some time, goes through this process.

There are several pieces of good news in all this. The first is, "Opportunity never sleeps." The second is, "There is always opportunity in chaos." Bad times are not necessarily total losses. How you react and manage those timely or untimely events will significantly impact your future. By that I mean if you learn to look for the silver lining in the storm clouds, you'll find opportunities and lessons where others can't.

"A pessimist sees the difficulty in every opportunity; an optimist sees the opportunity in every difficulty." ~ Winston S. Churchill

You've learned the most important basic's about money management — being aware of what your goals are and becoming conscious about your money and where you're spending it, and if how you spend is helping or hurting you. At least I hope you've learned that. You may or may not be feeling overwhelmed. I hope you're not feeling overwhelmed — we're just getting started!

Now that you're asking yourself if your spending is going to make you richer or poorer, let's move onto the foundational concept I like to call **S-P-A-R-C.**

S — START NOW

Warren Buffet calls Start Now the 'Noah Rule.' The 'Noah Rule' says: "Predicting rain doesn't count; building an ark does." In other words, don't just talk about it, do something to prepare for the future. Start building your ark today. If you're becoming mindful about whether or not your spending is going to make you richer or poorer, you've started. Pat yourself on the back. Now, back to the Noah Rule.

Buffett explained the Noah Rule in his 2001 shareholder report to ex-plain a big mistake he made when Berkshire Hathaway went through an awful year, further exacerbated by the events of 9/11. He explained that he'd actually predicted much of the market events before they happened, but he "didn't convert thought into action." In other words, he'd violated the 'Noah Rule' (the rains and floods came as he expected but he hadn't built an ark to escape them).

Whatever the financial journey you want to improve upon, make the commitment and take action *today*. For some of you reading this book that might be as simple as asking the 'richer or poorer' question. It might mean going further and creating a budget and learning discipline to stick with it. For others, it might mean hiring a full team of legal and financial experts and developing a complex plan that involves investments, estate planning, and more. Everyone is on a different path and at different places on their financial journey. Don't judge or compare yourself to anyone else. Focus on where you are, and on what you need to do next to reach your goals.

P — PLAN YOUR PROFESSIONAL TEAM

J. P. Morgan once said, "I do not pay my lawyers to tell me what I cannot do, but to tell me how to do what I want to do." That's excellent advice for us all. You'll have plenty of people telling you that you can't do what you envision. You need people telling you how you can make things happen, not trying to convince you that they won't happen.

If you're serious about your financial future, you will need to interview and hire the following at the very least: Hire a Fiduciary/ Fee Only Advisor or a Hybrid Advisor if needed. A Hybrid Registered Investment Advisor (RIA) is registered as both an RIA and Registered Representative of a broker/dealer or securities clearing firm. This dual registration allows advisors to operate both a Fee Only Practice for Asset Management and Financial Planning Service, as well as a commission-based practice that will pay the advisors based upon what product is sold.

There has always been controversy over commission only advisors when it comes to acting in the best interest of the client. So much so that the investment community of mutual fund companies and life insurance companies have gone to a levelized commission structure for consumers in order to eliminate those common practices of selling the highest commissioned products to their clients. In my opinion, a hybrid advisor is fine and well suited to offer a broad range of advice-driven strategies and solutions. If the Advisor is a "Fee Only" Registered Investment Advisor, he or she is retained in a Fee for Service only engagement. They are acting as a Fiduciary and obligated to adhere to the fiduciary standard. In other words, they have a legal obligation to always act in the best interest of their clients. You need to simply ask and always know which type of advisor you are engaging.

- An Accountant or CPA can guide you through the tax code and the tax planning process to avoid overpaying your taxes year after year.
- An Estate & Trust or Tax Attorney. Did you know that according to AARP, nearly 60% of Americans do not have a will or estate plan? Don't leave your end of life decisions to your spouse, children or worst of all, the court system.
- A CFP-Certified Financial Planner or CHFC-Chartered Financial Consultant can provide good overall financial planning advice. For business retirement plans, 401k implementation and reviews, hire someone with the following accreditation: AIF-Accredited Investment Fiduciary or an AIFA-Accredited Investment Fiduciary Analyst.
- A quality Banker and or a Mortgage Originator.
- A Seasoned Real Estate Professional. Whether you are buying your first home, investment or a commercial property you will likely need an experienced Realtor. In the years leading up to the great recession, many individuals bought more of a home than

they could afford by using high risk mortgage programs like interest only and reverse amortization loans, or "Low to No personal money down programs" as well as No Income-No Asset verification loans which were called accordingly, "Liar Loans " after the fact.

A — ADD YOUR FINANCIAL AND LEGAL TEAM

This should be done only after doing your research, educating yourself about various roles, and after interviews with each professional. If you've never interviewed a professional, don't worry. They expect it and want it. After all, they want to make sure they want to work with you as well. You're both building a relationship that you both want to last for a long time. This isn't an adversarial interview. Think of it as a first date. Is this someone you feel you can trust, who is authentic, skilled, and who will make a good business/financial partner?

You want to make sure they embrace the same values as you, your family and or business. Don't be afraid to replace someone if needed if you find out they're not a compatible match. I've had to replace people several times. It can be hard to cut someone from the team, but remember, this is your financial future at stake. You can't afford to have teammates who aren't contributing to your future. I mention legal because 60% of Americans have failed to do a basic will/estate plan. It might not seem that critical, but all kinds of unforeseen problems may arise for children, grandchildren and senior parents being cared for by children. When selecting an attorney for your financial team look for a finance lawyer.

Finance lawyers' expertise includes assisting clients with financial matters ranging from tapping debt markets to assisting corporations with restructuring businesses. Other specialized categories they handle may include banking, project finance, real estate finance and private equity finance, or they may have broad industry knowledge. It's important to know what you want them to do—whether help with drafting a will or estate plan, or assisting in other ways. You'll be hiring them, so they'll initially look to you for direction.

Why hire a lawyer before you need one? The cost of an attorney to keep you out of financial trouble is much less than the cost of one to get you *out* of trouble once you've made some poor choices.

Big law firm or solo practitioner? There are advantages and disadvantages to each. A larger firm will have every kind of specialist you might need under one roof. They'll cost more, but will save you time. A larger firm is going to have more influence, should you need that. They carry a bigger stick if they are large, well known, have attorneys in several states and are more networked. A solo attorney or someone from a small office will have fewer resources, less influence, and may not be able to practice in as many states. They will be less expensive. Don't forget that a larger firm may be able to make introductions to other resources such as alternative financing sources. They may also be able to make business introductions should you need that. Only you know which makes more sense for you.

R — RE-ESTABLISH AND REVIEW YOUR FINANCIAL GOALS WITH YOUR NEW "WEALTH TEAM'

One of the advantages of having a "team" of professionals to work with is you're exposed to ideas, possibilities, and expertise you never knew existed. Not only are you getting an objective view from your planner, but your team should be able to give you multiple perspectives on your financial plan and opportunities.

While each team member will be a different personality with different skill sets, they should all have one common characteristic—a legitimate interest in making sure your best interests come first. Trust your gut and intuition. Do your due diligence. Ask for their credentials and references and check them out.

These are the people you are trusting with your money, your future, and your life really. So take your time. You'll be glad you did. Even if a friend or business associate recommends them, check them out anyway. One of the things I found so interesting about Bernie Madoff's Ponzi scheme is that a lot of the people whose friends recommended him decided not to invest with him. They trusted their gut, followed what they knew, and recognized that what Madoff was promising didn't follow known return percentages.

When Madoff personally asked millionaire Donald Trump to invest with him, Trump turned him down, saying Madoff was a "sleaze and a total crook." Trump told CNN, "I would not, and a lot of my friends would not (invest with Madoff), but obviously a lot of my friends did. The word is very simple. It's a word called 'Greed.' That's all it was. People were greedy. They thought he was going to get them a greater return on their money. Obviously in hindsight this was an unrealistic assumption. I always tell my clients, "Don't allow fear or greed to control your financial decisions."

It's a basic rule we've all been taught since we were young: "If something sounds too good to be true, it probably is." I can think of dozens of clients and friends who, in spite of knowing better, opted into opportunities that sounded too good to be true, and unfortunately got burned. Like Trump said, "Greed." In our rush to get richer, do better, or make the deal of a lifetime, it's too easy to convince ourselves a fantastic opportunity is real when that intuitive side of us knows it's not. Listen to that voice and resist the temptation to act on the things your intuition tells you not to get involved with. There are risks, and then there is something beyond risk.

When you have a good, honest, reliable team they can help you avoid these risks, and pursue the ones that have promise. There's a difference. This is the kind of team you want—smart enough to recognize smart risks, and to support your dreams, but savvy enough to see problems and bad risks and alert you to the pros, cons, and potentially bad out-comes. Other than death and taxes, there are no sure things in life. Even the king of investing, Warren Buffett, will tell you that everyone, even experts like himself, make mistakes. The best simply make fewer mis-takes, know how to recover faster, and learn from their mistakes.

C — COORDINATE YOUR NEW GOALS AND STRATEGIES WITH YOUR WEALTH TEAM AND EDUCATE YOURSELF

Daymond John of *Shark Tank* is one of the most vocal financial masters to speak out about how critical it is to educate yourself about money. John secured a $300,000 order for FUBU (For You By You) hip-hop clothing startup. But, he was working out of his basement and needed to make $300,000 worth of clothes. It was his big break — only he didn't have the infrastructure, resources or financial knowledge to get the money. In fact, he was rejected for a loan by 27 banks! His mother interceded and took out an equity line on their home in Queens. It didn't get him the full loan, but got him $100,000 which he used to set up a mini-factory in the house. His worries were far from over. That $100,000 became $500. John was six months late on paying the mort-gage, and in danger of losing his mother's house.

He told CNBC reporter Catherine Clifford, "My lack of financial intel-ligence and my lack of having like-minded people around me was about to be my downfall." His mother told him she needed $2,000 to fix the problem. John went back to Red Lobster as a waiter, earned the money and gave it to his mother. She took out an ad in the local paper that said, "One million in orders needs financing." Okay, she stretched the truth, but she got results. Of the 33 people who responded to the ad, one— Samsung's textile division, was the real deal.

The company had been watching the urban clothing trend and wanted to test out the market. They made John an offer: They would fund his orders but he would have to make $5 million worth of sales in three years. John agreed. In just three months, he racked up $30 million worth of sales. Since then he's made it his mission to understand wealth, income, and money. He's made many mistakes since then, including losing $750,000 his first year on *Shark Tank*. But he's made more money than he's lost. He's not afraid to fail because he knows that's how we learn.[5]

Education comes in many forms. You can read books, take a class, join a group of like-minded investors, watch videos, listen to podcasts. Even if you have no time to read, you can learn while commuting to and from work, on your lunch break, or on weekends. If you're serious about learning (you're reading this book aren't you?) you will find or make time to educate yourself about wealth. Not every book about wealth will be about numbers and investing, percentages, and finance. A lot of helpful books will also be about the soft skills of life and money management.

Books like *Rich Dad, Poor Dad; Think and Grow Rich, The Millionaire Next Door* and *Your Money* or *Your Life* talk about our relationship with money. By relationship I mean how we *think* about money. What is our money mentality, how did we develop it and how can we change it? Understanding the tool that money is, is easy. Understanding the influence it has on our ego, our sense of self, our choice of career, how and what we spend our money on, is far more complex.

So when I say, "Educate yourself about money," I mean take time to examine your thoughts, feelings, and beliefs about money as well as learning how compounding, investing and budgets work. If you don't believe you deserve it, or are "worthy" of being wealthy or financially secure, you will sabotage yourself and any chance you have at achieving wealth—even if you consciously think you do deserve it!

---

[5] https://www.cnbc.com/2016/11/25/when-27-banks-rejected-daymond-john-his-mothers-advice-saved-him.html

Every money master I've researched and read says the same thing. Mindset matters.

"Your thoughts and feelings could play a part in how much money you earn. The biggest thing holding you back from building wealth is you," says Suze Orman, personal finance expert, best-selling author of *Women & Money* and host of the "Women and Money" podcast. Whether your fear keeps you from asking for a much-deserved raise, starting your business, or investing in your financial future, "everything", she says, "comes down to you thinking that you can't do it. You most likely are your own financial obstacle, and you have to remove your fears from wanting to create more," Orman told CNBC in a May 2019 interview about how your mindset could be holding you back from getting rich.

Other financial experts agree that your mindset can affect your finances. Jen Sincero, best-selling author of *You Are a Badass*, credits a shift in her financial mindset for her going from making $28,000 a year to making seven figures a year. Her advice comes from personal experience in being poor and being rich. She says that "the biggest difference between wealthy people and broke people is their mindset and how they feel about money."

Your mental money talk affects what and how you think. What you think affects how you feel. How you feel determines what decisions and actions you take. Eventually all those things combine to determine the financial results you get in every part of your life. By learning to recognize and then change that mental talk, you can change your life by changing how you feel, act, and what you believe about money. It sounds a little new age, but it's true. Even the Bible says so. Proverbs: 23:7: "For as he (man) thinketh in his heart, so is he."

CHAPTER TWO
AVOIDING FAILURE IN YOUR FINANCES — WHY PEOPLE ARE BAD AT MONEY MANAGEMENT.

"Someone's sitting in the shade today because someone planted a tree a long time ago. Successful investing takes time, discipline, and patience. No matter how great the talent or effort, some things take time." ~ Warren Buffett

People are bad at money management for three primary reasons:

- They have a lack of education about how money works and how to manage it.
- Their money mentality and their relationship with money.
- They lack the discipline to learn and incorporate money management skills into their lives.

EDUCATION

One of the things I'm constantly explaining to my clients is there's a distinct difference between your *income* and your *wealth*. Most of us use the terms interchangeably, at least when we're thinking about our money. But making money (your income), and accumulating/investing/managing money (your wealth), are two different things. You can have wealth even if you've lost your job and have no money (income). You can be poor even if you have a six-figure income and no savings (wealth). To avoid failure with your finances, you need to learn the difference between the two. Then you need to start learning how to manage both your income and your wealth.

In his book, *Profit First*, Mike Michalowicz shares how he learned that secret the hard way—literally burning through close to $300,000 dollars only to find he had had a great income, but no wealth. It inspired him to write his book about paying oneself first. Thus, the title.

How we *think* about money expands beyond the differences in income and wealth. It goes to our day-to-day money mentality. You don't have to believe me. Look at the lives of many of today's million and billionaires who have started poor and are finishing rich.

Ron Baron grew up in a house so small there was no room for a refrigerator inside, so they stored it on an outdoor porch. To help pay for college, Baron worked as a cabana boy, lifeguard, water-ski instructor and ice cream truck driver. He took $1,000 he saved from shoveling snow, waiting tables, working as a lifeguard, and selling ice cream, and turned it into $4,000 by investing in stocks.[6]

Daymond John is worth about $300 million dollars today, but as a young adult he lived and worked out of his mother's house. He started his fortune by converting $40 into $800 through making and selling caps. Then he turned that profit into a clothing line FUBU (For You By You) that eventually earned $350 million in sales in 1998. When that business slowed down, John created *Shark Tank*. He lost $750,000 the first season, but then it took off, making him millions.[7]

Financial guru and master Suze Orman chose to live in a van, work as a 'tree clearer' for a tree service, and then later wait tables for seven years—all while living in her van. She had no money to follow her

---

[6] https://www.app.com/story/money/business/2015/01/06/ron-baron/21334103/
[7] https://www.businessinsider.com/shark-tanks-daymond-john-mother-2015-5

dreams. Her parents couldn't help her, but customers she'd served for seven years at the Buttercup Cafe pooled their money to help her succeed. Hard work and her toughness, and entrepreneurial spirit led to her success.

Tony Robbins wasn't born with a silver spoon in his mouth, either. Yet he now owns a resort in Fiji, travels by private jet, and is an owner of Los Angeles' Major League Soccer team and has an estimated personal net worth of $500 million.[8] His Anthony Robbins company (a company of diverse businesses) makes a combined total of $6 billion a year. He made his first million at age 24. Before that he came from a broken home with a physically abusive mother, and worked as a janitor after school to help his family meet expenses. He says he wanted to 'become rich' as a child so he could 'help people,' and he's done that.

During the holiday season, The Anthony Robbins Foundation feeds more than four million people annually through its international "Basket Brigade," and provides fresh water to over 100,000 people a day in India, where water-borne disease is the leading cause of death for children. The foundation runs programs to help the homeless, encourage youth leadership, and provide his books and tapes to prisoners.[9]

MONEY MINDSET

People are bad at money management for a lot of reasons, but the experts and I believe one of the most overlooked reasons for people's failures around money, income, and wealth is their mindset—how they think, and feel about money, and what their beliefs about money are. The five primary kinds of mindsets about money are:

---

[8] https://wealthygorilla.com/tony-robbins-net-worth/
[9] https://www.businessinsider.com/tony-robbins-life-story-2015-6#he-travels-exclu-sively-by-private-jet-and-says-it-has-changed-his-productivity-more-than-anything-on-earth-theres-nothing-that-changes-quality-of-life-when-you-travel-as-much-as-i-do-as-that-he-told-the-so-money-podcast-11

- Poverty Mentality
- Entitled Mentality
- Necessary Evil Mentality
- Scarcity Mentality
- Positive Money Mentality

There are more, and most of us with financial issues have one or more of these mindsets. Do you have a poverty mindset and don't know it? Millions of people do, and it holds them back more than any other thing they have going on. No matter how much they make, or how they save, they just can't seem to get ahead.

You don't have to be homeless, poor or impoverished to have a poverty mentality. There are, surprisingly enough, many millionaires with a poverty mentality. I knew a woman, Sally, who was a multimillionaire. She drove a 30-year old Fiat, never tipped more than a dollar on any meal, even those restaurant meals for a family of six that came to $200 dollars or more. Her house was modest, and the furniture she had when she died was still circa 1965 when she bought it. Her four daughters ran the gamut from penny pincher to wild spender according, it seemed to me, how she raised each. She was financially strict with the two oldest, who followed her financial style, and more generous with the youngest, who didn't save or manage money as well as their older siblings.

TIP: Our money mentality often has little to do with our current financial status, and everything to do with how we were raised around money and what we learned to believe about it.

"Fear and doubt destroy more dreams than failure ever does. Most people don't live their dreams; they live their fears."
~ Keith Weinhold

A poverty mentality or mindset (or any mindset really) is simply a collection of beliefs about money, such as: believing that money shouldn't be spent, that opportunities are limited and any risk at all is dangerous. Some of us believe that we shouldn't be generous because any success is temporary and non-replicable. These folks subscribe to a policy that remaining in the back of the pack is generally the safest way to live. Is that depressing or what? I'm not saying spend your money frivolously. But I am saying that your attitude and beliefs about money play a huge role in how you earn, save, spend, invest and most importantly, enjoy your money.

Fear of money, a lack of financial discipline, a failure to budget, or to have a spending plan, can contribute to losing control of your finances. Frivolously overspending it, gambling it away or losing it to high interest credit card debt, all contribute to our feeling out of control of our money. So why do so many people fail in their finances even after they start budgeting, saving, and getting more control over their money? Without a doubt I believe it's their mindset or money mentality. How we think, behave, and interact with our money is psychological, emotional, and probably learned behavior from our family upbringing. The poverty mindset is the most common, but we can have beliefs from all five mindsets.

Napoleon Hill, one of my favorite financial masters, said that the single most important thing a person can develop in their lifetime is a positive attitude. "No other trait, not experience, not knowledge will produce as much for you as a positive, enthusiastic attitude. It can create miracles for you. Ninety percent of winning in life," Hill says, "Is always being excited. The key to staying excited is to lead by example. Happy people attract others like them, and negative, frustrated people do too. Negative people drain your batteries, so practice a positive attitude. Everybody loves to be around positive people. Being a positive person doesn't happen overnight. It's okay to get down, discouraged, and depressed, but only as long as you do it for a short time each day, and never in front of others."[10] Is success that simple? I think it can be. A positive attitude definitely changes your outlook on life. Consider Todd:

"It's like I'm cursed," Todd, aged 55, told me. Todd is a construction foreman, considered himself a big dreamer, a ladies' man of sorts, and a savvy businessman. The fact was his dreams (like his construction business) had never come to fruition. He'd had many girlfriends, but never had a stable relationship, let alone making it to the wedding altar. In his 30s, when his business struggled to meet payroll at least once a month during a slow season, he eventually gave up his business and got a job. He was afraid of failing and hated the anxiety and fear he felt during those times. He couldn't see that once he got through the slow season things always picked up again. Some people look for the silver lining in the clouds, Todd hunted down thunderstorms and looked for the darkest clouds and deepest pits he could find to justify his money mentality. It was almost an obsession with him. He seemed driven to prove that he wasn't worthy of whatever it was he thought he wanted.

Todd wasn't cursed. He wasn't wallowing in poverty. He was single, and he made $100,000 a year. He wasn't really hurting for money. He just had a poverty mindset about his money. Not only that, his entire family, his father and mother, and his siblings all had the same mindset. What Todd and his family believed about money was:

- No matter how hard I work I can never make ends meet.
- No matter how hard I work I never have enough money.
- I'll never make enough money.
- I'll always be broke.
- Nothing ever works out for me so why bother trying?
- I never get a break.
- I can't afford it.
- That's for rich people, not me.
- Everyone else has more money than me.

10

- If I didn't have bad luck, I'd have no luck at all.
- I can't afford milk and bread, let alone a vacation!
- Everyone else gets all the breaks.

In addition to these beliefs, Todd and his family were jealous of others who seemed to have more than they did. They took it personally when they saw friends driving a new car, or even a new used car, or posting photos of their camping vacations on Facebook! They focused on what they didn't have, not on what they did have. They self-sabotaged, and were generally negative when it came to money, possessions, and their jobs. Even though Todd could have easily afforded to take a vacation, he thought it was frivolous to spend money on himself. He lived in a modest house, drove a used pickup truck, and was frugal far beyond what he had to be. His savings and 401K, and his retirement plan were in great shape, but not in his mind. Yes, you can have a lot of money and still feel and believe you have 'no' money.

For instance, Todd told me he'd been approached by a company, a competitor, who offered him a job. It was making higher end six-figures, overseeing men in the field, traveling, and with more responsibility— his dream job. Yet, he turned down the offer, telling me the company probably just wanted to get him away from his current job (which he hated) so they could "screw with him."

I initially felt like I had to show him the door. Instead, however, I suggested that he talk to a therapist to get at the roots of his negativity around money and work. He wanted the job, but didn't believe he deserved it, or that he would be able to keep up with the extra demands of travel and new people. He was afraid and yet angry at himself for being afraid. His family also contributed to his decision, reinforcing his belief that he wasn't skilled enough or good enough to do the job.

Like most people with a poverty mindset, Todd didn't have the self-esteem to believe in himself. He had grown up around parents who struggled to make a living (and who still struggled!). He learned, as we all do, from seeing and hearing what those around him believed about money. Todd would need to deliberately change his mindset, his environment and his beliefs to see his life, and his income, change and get better.

ENTITLED MENTALITY

The "entitled" mentality has always been around, but nowhere nearly as often and as aggressively as we've seen in the last few decades. The entitled mentality is one of "I'm owed. I deserve it. I shouldn't have to work for it. People should just give it to me." It's the mindset that privileges are rights. It fosters a belief that you aren't responsible for your financial status, that others are. It allows people to focus on who or what to blame rather than the role they're playing in their own financial health. The entitled mentality (financial or otherwise) means a person is also unwilling to accept the consequences for their actions, as in: "I deserve this car/house/wardrobe/dinner so I'm buying it. I shouldn't have to worry about paying my rent/mortgage/utility bills, so I won't."

Entitled individuals begin to lean more and more on the government or other agencies to bail them out or rescue them. They never learn to take control of their own finances, and eventually find themselves in a very deep hole that they've dug for themselves. It's the college student who graduates and assumes they'll immediately be hired into a six-figure job even though they have no experience, no credentials other than a degree, and no connections or assets to bring to the table. Then they blame others that they're working minimum wage jobs, or that 'no one' will hire them to run a multi-million-dollar corporation even though they can't even balance their checkbooks.

As Wikipedia says about entitled persons, "They misinterpret the Declaration of Independence's affirmation of their *right to pursue* happiness as a *Constitutional guarantee of* happiness."

NECESSARY EVIL MENTALITY

Something that has always fascinated me is the "money is a necessary evil" mentality. It reminds me of a refrigerator magnet I once saw. It read, "Some people think having no money makes them more spiritual, others think having more money makes them more blessed."

Whichever position you take goes back to religion and people believing that God blesses the righteous financially, and punishes the unrighteous with poverty. I don't want to get into who is right or wrong, but I do want to point out that both righteous and unrighteous people are rich, poor, and everything in between. As the Bible says, "God maketh His sun to rise on the evil and on the good, and sendeth rain on the just and on the unjust." ~ Matthew 5:45.

If you have a "money is a necessary evil" mentality, chances are you're seeing money as an indicator of character, or spirituality, and not as a tool. You realize that money makes the world go round and that you have to have it if you want the luxuries and necessities of life, but you resent it. You wish there was some way to get what you want without dealing with money and the issues and challenges that come with it.

You're welcome to think of money any way you want, but if you see it as something undesirable, dirty, or spiritually demeaning, you're going to have a harder time managing it.

SCARCITY MENTALITY

Tom, a golfing friend of mine, called to cancel a golf game we had scheduled. His parents had received an eviction notice and called him, begging for his help. Shocked, he was on his way over to find out what happened. They owned their home outright, and he had no idea what might have happened to them.

What he saw when he got there stunned him. His parents were hoarders. He hadn't been in the house in years as they always wanted to celebrate holidays with him and his wife and kids at his house, not theirs. "No need to drag everyone over here," his parents had said. "We'll come over to your house; it's bigger anyway and the kids won't have to leave their friends."

He learned then that their protests were all part of hiding their hoarding. But they couldn't hide it from everyone. Neighbors had complained and eventually the health department filed the paperwork to have them evicted and the house cleared out and torn down.

"I don't understand it," he told me. "They were holding onto broken fans and appliances, old newspapers, and empty pizza boxes. I walked through the house pointing to things and they kept telling me, 'We might use it one day.'"

What Tom was seeing in his parents was the far end of the scarcity mentality spectrum—a mental disorder known as hoarding.

A scarcity mindset is the belief that there will never be enough—whether it's money, food, emotions or something else entirely. A scarcity mindset can cause people to hoard or save money, or to never let go of things and physical property they have for fear of needing them someday, but not being able to afford them if they did. Not everyone with a scarcity mindset is a hoarder. Some may save everything and live like paupers on a six-figure income.

I was told about a man in Virginia who owned thousands of acres of land, but was unable to pay the taxes on one particular piece of property in a growing area. He could have sold an acre of another, less popular 20-acre property he had in order to pay the back taxes on this property, but wouldn't. The last I heard the county was in the process of seizing the land. His scarcity mentality was such that he would lose 40-acres because he couldn't bear to part with a parcel of just a couple of acres so that he could pay the taxes.

A few years ago I read a story about a man named Dan Price. The last name is ironic. Price was a successful Kentucky photojournalist, but he was also a very stressed out family man with a wife and two kids. In 2013, at the age of 33 he walked away from his life, his job, and his family. He moved to Oregon, where he was from originally, and dug himself a hole in the ground under a horse pasture. He built a tiny "hob-bit house" in the hole and has been living there for more than 20 years. I would find that incredibly stressful. Dan doesn't. In fact, he no longer stresses about money. He lives on $5,000 a year, pays $100 a year for rent on the two acres of land he lives on, and he writes about money and sells his books at his blog http://www.moonlightchronicles.com/. People may deny themselves any simple or reasonable expenditures for fear of needing the money or possessions someday. Hoarding may be the extreme end of the spectrum of scarcity, but the foundational fear of not having enough is the same.

While I was doing the research for this book and relating this story, someone told me about Sue, their sister. Sue was 72, active, healthy, intelligent, lived alone on a small farm, and yet owned four ironing boards and six irons. "I don't think she's ironed anything in 30 years," this person said.

"And why does she need four ironing boards and six irons?"

In interviewing Sue I learned that she had once been an executive assistant for a large oil company. Her wardrobe then consisted of very expensive, immaculately ironed suits and blouses—many of which she still owned, but never wore.

When she was working she ironed everything herself, and would set up her outfit on several boards at once so she didn't have to keep switching out the items. The irons were set on the proper settings for silk, wool, and cotton and she never changed them for fear of burning or scorching her expensive outfits. Now all the ironing boards and irons made sense! But she hadn't had to iron anything in decades. All she wore now, out of choice, were t-shirts, flannel shirts, and sweaters and jeans because well, she lives on a working farm.

"I guess I keep them out of habit," she confessed. "I think someone is going to call me up and want me in a meeting and I'll need to iron something." She laughed.

"How silly is that! "The next month she called me to tell me she gave away all but one ironing board and one iron. "I probably won't ever use them," she confessed. "But I might."

You laugh at the absurdity of that many ironing boards and irons. What I found interesting about Sue's scarcity mentality was that like many of us she believed that "someday something would happen and she'd need her irons and ironing boards." I know of people who laugh at this story, yet they themselves hold onto golf clubs, sporting equipment, camping equipment, and even old cars that don't run. We seem to be a society of believers and dreamers. We believe that "someday" we'll need something and won't be able to afford to buy it if and when we do. Even in the face of the fact we're more likely to win the lottery than be asked to return to a job we left 25 years ago, we still hold onto things. Even if the likelihood we'll be invited to sail around the world and will need a full set of foul weather rain gear for the journey is absolutely zero, we hold onto the gear "just in case."

Most of us don't believe we'll have the money to buy newer, working versions of what we're holding onto should we need it. But I believe most of us hold onto the items we never use because by letting go of the item, we're also letting go of the dream that we will use them. If someone gives up their downhill skis and snowsuit they're admitting they'll never downhill ski again, even though it's been 40 years since they have.

One of my researchers for this book was telling me about her parents. "They have enough canned goods in the basement to open a grocery store," she said.

"The only problem is, more than half of the cans are expired and the food is no good."

When people have a scarcity mentality they fail to see how much money they waste by trying to avoid not having what they might need one day. It makes sense to have a week or two of food and water on hand if you live in a natural disaster-prone area where you won't get much notice of an impending disaster. But there's not much sense in stocking up for a five-year apocalypse.

When you have a scarcity mindset, instead of believing that you have enough, and that there is plenty to go around, you cling to everything you have out of fear of coming up short.

It's not just wasting money you do have. A scarcity mindset keeps you from making money you might otherwise make. When you're focused on what you don't have, you don't think about what you could have, or on other opportunities around you. Fear of not having enough holds you back, so like Todd, the construction manager, you settle for working for someone else for much less rather than take risks and pursue building your own business. You put off making decisions in case something else comes along. You prefer to put that $20 or $40 aside for an unexpected bill instead of going for coffee or dinner with a friend when you really do have enough money to enjoy a night out.

Another "scarcity mentality" I want to discuss is the one where people tell you to "live below your means." Robert Kiyosaki says, "The classic mantra to 'live below your means' is one of the most destructive things you can teach someone about money. It teaches people to think in terms of scarcity. You only have so much, so you must be careful not to run out." He shares the story of his 'rich dad, poor dad' example.

"Growing up my poor dad would always say, 'I can't afford that.' My rich dad, however, would ask the question, 'How *can* I afford that?' One way of thinking, my poor dad's way, sees a world of scarcity. My rich dad would see a world of abundance. Instead of living below your means, how can you find a way to increase your means?"

I'm not saying I agree with spending everything you earn (Parkinson's Law), but I also don't think living below your means to the point you're miserable, or denying yourself the fruits of your labor is wise. I think in some cases it can be detrimental. Financial master Mike Michalowicz has a unique approach to this situation, one he calls *Profit First*. He believes that we should find a financial point at which we're comfortable (our profit) and pay ourselves first, then pay our expenses. Most business owners and people follow a formula of:

Income Minus Expenses = Profit.

That means profit is what we get to keep after we've paid for everything else, be it operating expenses, salaries, and taxes or mortgage, utilities, and car repairs. The problem, he explains, is that the bigger we grow, the more our expenses grow too. It becomes a never-ending cycle that keeps our profitability at bay and keeps our businesses or financial life unhealthy. "It's kind of like saying, my health comes last." he says. It also shuts down our ability to find creative solutions to pay for/barter or come up with the money for expenses. "We lose that ability, we dumb down things once the money is there," he explains. "Rather than think, how can I come up with a way to pay for this we just take it out of our money." That might seem logical and reasonable - and the way most of us do things. But, then I'm reminded of Cordia Harrington, known as the "Bun Lady."

Harrington owns the Tennessee Bun Company. She says her company makes 1,000 buns a minute, 60,000 buns an hour — more buns per hour than anybody else on the planet.

But being a baker isn't where she started. Her career as a realtor and her openness to possibility is what ultimately led her to becoming the most well-known baker in America. Even as a realtor her beginnings were humble. She needed an office, but couldn't afford it, so she bartered for it. She bartered for her office, and leased her desk and chairs. And she went from there, spotting a real estate opportunity in buying a McDonald's franchise. She knew what all entrepreneurs learn, that necessity is the mother of invention. When that necessity is no longer there, we can get creatively soft — and stop seeing opportunities that we might otherwise recognize. If there was an opportunity in her world, Harrington followed it.

For instance, she noticed that riders from the Greyhound Bus were a large part of her McDonald's franchise business, so she bought a Greyhound bus franchise and built a bus-stop at the edge of her McDonald's parking lot to ensure that she always had customers.[11] Starting out with just $587 in her pocket, she's built herself a $100 million bun empire.[12] She didn't let naysayers get the best of her either.

When confronted with discrimination by her male colleagues for being a woman she dressed up in a man's suit and tie and argued her business to her board as a man. They laughed, but she got what she wanted. Keeping that creative edge is important if you want to succeed and to continuously recognize opportunities around you.

To ensure you don't lose your creative edge, Michalowicz says a better way to see or manage your money is to allocate your "profit first" rather than let your expenses and operating costs determine how much money you get. The premise is to allocate a percentage of the income on the front end for profit. It looks like this:

Income Minus Profit = Expenses.

That simple shift "reverse engineers your profitability," he says.

---

[11] https://premierespeakers.com/cordia-harrington/bio
[12] https://www.insideedition.com/headlines/9985-with-587-in-her-pocket-she-built-a-100-million-empire-on-buns

"It takes courage and dedication to stick with it," he writes, "But the payoff is worth it." The details for how to do this are in Mike's book, *Profit First*. It's a great read and, as with all the financial master's books, I suggest you buy it and study it.

POSITIVE OR MIDAS MONEY MENTALITY

People who have an abundance mindset feel very positive about their money. They trust their ability to make and manage it. Some people call this a millionaire or Midas mindset. They look at those who have this mindset and say, "Everything they touch turns to gold." While it might seem that these people are "lucky," or "gifted," the truth is they've simply developed a habit of thinking that results in this mindset. They:

- Forgive themselves for their financial failures and mistakes, learn from them, and move on. They don't constantly remind themselves of their past or past failings.
- They don't compare themselves with others. Keeping up with the Jones' used to be how people thought of this bad habit. Now it's "keeping up with Facebook, "and the things and lifestyles people see on social media. Don't do it.
- They have good money habits. You'll learn about these same habits throughout the book. Practice them and you too can develop good money habits.
- They practice gratitude. Laugh if you want but keeping a gratitude journal has been shown to not only improve your mood, but your contentment with what you have. Many of those who practice daily expressions of gratitude see their income and their wealth increase. You have nothing to lose by doing the same.
- *"When you are grateful fear disappears and abundance appears."* ~ Tony Robbins

STEER CLEAR OF THE POVERTY MINDSETS OF OTHERS

"Never take financial advice from a poor man or a business owner who just filed for bankruptcy." You'd think this would be obvious, but it's not. If someone giving you financial advice is living paycheck-to-paycheck, chances are they don't know what they're talking about in terms of money management. Or, even if they do, they don't have the skills or discipline to apply what they know to their own money. If they can't manage and invest their own money, do you really want to trust them with your financial fortune, however large or small it might be?

I remember a limo driver in late 1999 giving me advice on internet stocks on one of my trips to the Philadelphia airport. The Dot.Com boom was in a full-blown irrational exuberance trend. You literally could throw a dart at any dot com stock in those days and make money. During that time, I remember a discussion with one of my friends, Rick, who I started with in the business back in 1984. We were both wondering if financial advisors would still be sought after in the years ahead since everyone was earning double digit returns with literally no effort, no education and no market downside seen in years.

Needless to say, a year later there was a devastating development for these stocks as the Nasdaq composite started a 3-year decline and many dot com darlings went bankrupt. The Nasdaq lost 39.29% in 2000, 21.05 % in 2001, and 31.53% in 2002. Talk about a painful storm.

More recently while I was visiting Washington DC, my wife and I Ubered downtown along with some friends. After some small talk the driver realized what I did for a living and started to tell me how he was investing in various crypto currencies. Really?

All I will say is that I've only met one individual that admitted to buying some Bitcoin for under 1,000.00. The rest I've known who bought between $10,000-$18,000 per coin obviously aren't talking so loud about their cryptocurrency experience and the major swings or losses they have incurred.

There's a difference in listening to the financial advice of others if you're in a financial club where everyone is learning about investing, and the point of offering advice is to learn from each other. It doesn't make any sense to go to a financial advisor working out of the trunk of his car, or neighbors or family members who are asking to borrow money for rent while at the same time telling you how to invest or manage your money.

Even if your friends are having some success with their investments, you can't build your success around their example. Yes. Study and watch what they're doing, but understand why it's working so you can make informed, educated decisions for yourself and your financial goals.

Mental health experts tell me we're the sum of the top five people we spend time with. If you're spending time with people who are working hard and trying to become better at what they do, or just better people, chances are that's your mindset too. If you're spending most of your time with people who come home and hang out in front of the television before going to bed, well — you're probably doing the same. That old saying, "Birds of a feather flock together," is true. You don't find many eagles hanging out with turkeys. Look around. What kind of social circle are you in?

ASSOCIATE WITH SUCCESS

> *"Most people fail in life because they major in minor things."*
> -Tony Robbins

Chances are you're not going to go out and find a millionaire to rub elbows with after reading this book. But, stranger things have happened. One of the things you must do is look at with who you're spending the majority of your time (spouses count). We really are a reflection of the company we keep. If you want to be smarter, associate with smart people. The type of people you surround yourself with speaks of your values and what you stand for, but it also determines your attitudes about success, money, and money management. If you're associating with people who live paycheck-to-paycheck, guess what your money mentality is going to be? That's right—paycheck-to-paycheck. Find people around you, at school, church, meetup groups, etc. who have the kind of money mentality you want to have. Once you tap into that network you'll find more like-minded people who will inspire you to up your game as well.

HAVE A GOAL

"Once your values are clear your financial decisions become easy,"
~ David Bach

If you're reading this book, you're thinking about your money situation—whether it's good or bad. You're probably exploring ways to improve it, or at least stop the hemorrhaging of cash. Maybe you're in a place where you can take time to think about your financial future, or maybe you're desperate, looking for a quick fix. No matter where you are, you still need a goal before you can move forward, make decisions or take action.

If you're young, still in high school, college, or postgraduate school, you may or may not be thinking of your future 50 years down the road. But this is actually the best time to be doing exactly that!

If you're in your mid-30s, 40s, or even 50s, it's definitely time to be thinking about your future. The problem is, so many of us are so busy working, paying bills and living paycheck-to-paycheck or are so consumed with the pressures of just living life that we don't take time to sit down, focus, and PLAN. Therein lies the secret to financial planning, says Bach. He continues, "No one has time or discipline. You have to set plans up to be automatic. The entire secret to saving is automation. When people save automatically, for college or to buy a home or re-tire—or all of the above—they actually get it done."

Of course I'd advise people to hire a financial planner! I am one! But David Bach also recommends people hire an advisor.

"Once you have $100,000 or more, you should hire a financial advisor—especially once you are in your 50s. Hire a fiduciary, a registered in-vestment advisor who can provide a written financial plan. You want a clear understanding of how much money you have, taxes, Social Secu-rity, where your income will come from and how long it will last," he told *Forbes* writer Jennifer Barret in a 2018 interview.

BORING IS BEST

When it comes to investing, forget all the hype, excitement, and frenzy you've seen in Hollywood movies. Real investing isn't like that, and when it is, the down side is just as intense. When it comes to investing, Bach says "Boring is really good. Have a diversified portfolio with stocks and bonds. When it comes to your money, boring is really good." I concur.

DON'T JUST FOLLOW YOUR FRIEND OR FAMILY'S ADVICE

Your financial success can't be built around your best friend's or your neighbor's, or your family's financial success—even if they are doing well with their investments. It's got to be done on a personalized level. You can't just copy your neighbor's portfolio. Well, you can, but it's so much better for you if you have your own portfolio based on your unique goals, values, and investment risk tolerances.

One of the best parts of this book is that it touches on the variety of advice from the money masters. While all these experts have arrived at their success through a variety of paths and philosophies, there are many points and paths on which they all agree — like budgeting, saving, paying yourself first, and losing your poverty mindset. This book is about finding, relating, connecting, and sharing those common points so that you see where they agree. That's what's most important.

If one person recommends something to you and they have influence in the money space, that's one thing. But when three people share the same advice, that means so much more than the sum of its parts. Sometimes the advice people give won't be couched in the same terms, but the intent or practice is the same. Three such examples I like to share come from non-financial experts. This piece of advice is about risk and change:

A pastor named Thomas S. Monson wrote about risk, and change, and opportunity in a blog post I read recently—"There is no tomorrow to remember if we don't do something today." He then related a story Arthur Gordon wrote in a national magazine, and I quote:

"When I was around thirteen and my brother ten, Father had promised to take us to the circus. But at lunchtime there was a phone call; some urgent business required his attention downtown. We braced ourselves for disappointment. Then we heard him say [into the phone], 'No, I won't be down. It'll have to wait.'

"When he came back to the table, Mother smiled. She said, "The circus keeps coming back, you know.'

"'I know,' said Father. 'But childhood doesn't.'"

The lesson there, I believe, is to consider all the opportunities before us, be they financial or personal, and to think of the impact they will have on our financial and personal futures. Some decisions will be financial, others will be more personal. It's up to you to decide what to build and how to build it.

Warren Buffett encourages seriously considering what you can do today in order to have a return on tomorrow (future). Through the years, there are people who have not done enough of this thinking, or they wait too long to act even if they do consider it. You could be on one or the other side of this. You either wait too long or you'll move too fast.

Many of my clients wait too long, and then they're always trying to play catch up. I always like to say that it's never too late to start. For example, I knew the owner of a local printing company. He was 61 years old, married to a younger spouse, and was always afraid to invest any money in any financial instruments other than a savings or money market account.

One of the things he asked me was, "Jay, is it too late for me? Did I wait too long? I know I should have started doing some of these things 20 years ago."

I told him like I'll tell you, "It's never too late to start." No, you probably won't make the same gains you would have if you started investing at age 21 or if your parents started investing for you at birth. However, if you are the type of person who has waited for a long time, that shouldn't stop you from looking at where you are today, evaluating where you are, and then seeing what steps you can take to improve on your current situation.

I heard a quote many years ago that goes, "People don't plan to fail in life or their finances. They just fail to plan." That's what I believe Buffett was referring to. Investing takes time. It takes discipline, and it's not a one-time decision. It's not a, "I'm going to do my planning this year," and then forget about it for five or ten years and never make a change, never make an adjustment.

That's where people make their biggest mistake. They fail to see their money and their relationship with it as a living breathing thing that must be tended to regularly — like any relationship. They need to continually improve on the groundwork that they've laid for their finances and they've got to be disciplined and passionate about it. Like anything in life, things don't normally happen quickly. Most of the millionaires out there today will tell you that it took time, effort, discipline and nurturing their finances to get to where they are today. In this book, we're going to focus on what it takes to achieve some of those levels of success.

DON'T BE AFRAID TO FAIL

One of the things I frequently hear from both friends and clients is, "But what if I'm wrong? What if I fail?"

I remind them that if investing were an exact science, everyone would be a Warren Buffet and we'd all be rich. The fact is, investing is not an exact science. It's a contradictory one. John Kenneth Gailbraith once said, "In economics, the majority is always wrong!" But then again, history has shown the majority is often right. When do you know which way to take the "path less traveled" versus the "broad and worn public thoroughfare"?

Hopefully the tips in this book will help you decide. I promise you, the answers for your financial plan won't be the same answers your friend gets. But, you'll both get the same information to help you make your investment decisions! One of the most fascinating articles I came across when doing research for this book was on Warren Buffet's financial regrets. There were 15 very specific regrets (along with the lessons he learned) in the article. I found it amazing to realize he had made some pretty poor decisions. There's a link to the article at the end of this book, but here are two of the most impressive lessons Buffet learned were:

One: Don't make financial decisions based on anger, spite, or vindictiveness.

I can't tell you how common this is, this desire to "show somebody" or "prove something" or extract revenge in a financial way, be it divorce, investing, or buying or selling property. In a 2010 interview with Becky

Quick on CNBC, Warren Buffett said the dumbest stock he ever bought was Berkshire Hathaway, but the dumbest thing he ever *did* with the company was to be vindictive about "punishing" a company manager.

Buffett said he first invested in Berkshire Hathaway in 1962. At the time it was a failing textile company. He believed it would begin making a profit when more mills closed, so he loaded up on the stock. Later, he says, the firm tried to chisel him out of more money. Angry and spiteful Buffett bought control of the company. He then fired the manager and tried to keep the textile business running for another 20 years. Now Buffett estimates this petty, vindictive move cost him $200 billion.

Two: Get input from people you trust before making major investments. In his 2008 shareholders letter, Buffett wrote, "Without urging from Charlie or anyone else, I bought a large amount of ConocoPhillips stock when oil and gas prices were near their peak. I in no way anticipated the dramatic fall in energy prices that occurred in the last half of the year."

Buffett explains he spent just over $7 billion on 85 million shares of ConocoPhillips, but its market value at the time of the letter was only about $4.4 billion.

Mistakes like this only emphasize the importance of consulting people you trust before making a major investment. That difference of perspective can often bring up issues, problems, or facts you aren't aware of.

Remember, investing isn't a mathematical certainty. It's both science and art, but mostly art. There's a lot at play in investing decisions. There are times and opportunities even in the worst of times that can be your golden ticket—if you know what to look for. If you don't believe that, then look at one of the most stunning successes of the last century — Airstream trailers. Of more than 400 travel trailer builders operating in 1936, Airstream was the only one to survive the Great Depression years. They didn't survive because they were the cheapest. They survived because their founder, Wally Byam was focused on quality and on his customers. Did he understand money and how people related to it? He did. Like many other investors and rich men, Byam started off poor. By the time he graduated from high school both his mother and stepfather had died, leaving him orphaned and with not much money. His poverty wouldn't last. By the time the Great Depression was in full swing in 1931, Byam decided to start his camping trailer business. His first unit the Clipper, sold at $1200, and was considered an expensive travel trailer. However, market response to the product was so strong Byam's company could not build units fast enough to satisfy the deluge of orders. Even during a recession, a depression, and hard economic times, it's possible to make and save money.[13]

I have a belief, "Opportunity never sleeps" regardless of the economic cycle we may be in. Remember the conversation about wise investing I mentioned earlier with Jimmy? I told him the same thing I'm telling you now: "Like Wally Byam, sometimes you've got to take a contrarian look at things."

I went further, asking Jimmy, "For example, right now, what asset out there does no one want to own?" At the time we were talking about this, the answer was real estate.

If you look back at real estate in '07 you'll understand why people were panicking, worried and getting out of real estate. The United States was experiencing a real estate housing bubble that affected over half of the U.S. states. Housing prices began to peak in early 2006, then quickly fell off, declining in 2006 and 2007. On December 30, 2008, the Case–Shiller home price index reported its largest price drop in its history. It wasn't just houses that were dropping. So were credit scores. The credit crisis resulting from the housing bubble burst is an important cause of the 2007–2009 recession in the United States. Banks were collapsing,

---

[13] https://en.wikipedia.org/wiki/Wally_Byam

people who had six-figure incomes were becoming homeless. It was a nightmare for millions.

People who bought their home in those years were underwater. Their real estate was really low. If you had the insight and the money to say, "Now might be a great time to be investing in real estate because nobody wants it and it's cheap," you'd likely be pretty rich today depending on where and what you purchased. Always remember the favorite real estate saying, "It's Location, Location, Location".

The same thing happened with the stock market. For example, the Dow Industrial hit a low of 5600 in March 2009. In March 2019, approximately 10 years later, it hit 26,000. When would you have loved to have money in the market? It would have been late 2008 and Spring of 2009 when everyone was selling the market, and nobody wanted to own it.

Do you see the common theme here? Having money when people are fearful is a good time to make smart investments. Warren Buffet was quoted during the Great Recession, "Be Fearful when everyone is greedy and Greedy when everyone is fearful". The lesson is, "Don't take all of your money and throw it into any one investment idea or strategy. Use a well-balanced asset allocation model in an effort to spread your risk over various asset classes. That combination should include Large, Medium & Small Cap Equities, Short, Long and Intermediate term Government & Corporate Bonds, International Sectors, Real estate & Alternative Asset Classes or "AAC" for short. Another term synonymous with AAC would be a Hedge Fund Asset Class strategy and or Non-Correlating Investment Assets like Gold, Silver or even Art.

If you are really looking to have upside growth with Zero risk to principal, you can always consider an Indexed or Fixed Annuity. However, compare carefully for those with zero fees, shorter holding periods and the highest credit ratings from A.M. Best or Moody's.

Having said that, it is advisable to talk to your Fiduciary Advisor within your SPARC team, which we will cover in Chapter 9.

While making the right investments it is important to know you can't do that without three things:

- **Money.** You have to pay to play and having money is the first step in ensuring you're ready to act when opportunity arises
- **Education**. Becoming educated creates confidence in your financial future and helps you make the right informed decisions.
- **Experts.** You don't have to have a personal posse of experts in all fields (real estate, etc.) around you at all times, but finding and hiring the right people to advise and assess your personal or business situation is critical. It ensures you don't overstep your self-acquired knowledge when making complex decisions. Find and build a relationship with these experts before you need them, not when you're in a crunch financially or timewise.

Buffett makes it a practice to never invest in anything he doesn't understand. "You have to learn how to value businesses and know the ones that are within your circle of competence and the ones that are outside," Buffett says.[14]

That's because it's crucial for investors to be able to confidently assess the businesses they hold. "Intelligent investing is not complex, though that is far from saying that it is easy. What an investor needs is the ability to correctly evaluate selected businesses. Note that word 'selected': You don't have to be an expert on every company, or even many. You only have to be able to evaluate companies within your circle of competence.

"The size of that circle is not very important; knowing its boundaries, however, is vital," he said in his 1996 annual shareholder's letter.[15]

---

[14] https://www.inc.com/david-cancel/charlie-munger-warren-buffett-use-this-mental-model-to-stay-focused-on-their-strengths.html
[15] https://www.berkshirehathaway.com/letters/1996.html

DISCIPLINE

Last, but certainly not least of the three reasons people struggle with money is that while they may learn and identify what they need to know, they still struggle to change their mindset about money. They discover they don't really have the discipline to implement those changes into their lives. They try, and fail, and then try again, fail again, and give up.

If you've ever seen a magazine with healthy models with six-pack abs, and gleaming, toned and tan bodies flexing their muscles and wished you had the same, you're not alone. We all want those bodies, just like so many of us envy Warren Buffet's 84-billion-dollar net worth. The thing is, body builders didn't get those bodies after a day, or a week or even months at the gym. And it's taken Buffett a lifetime to amass his earnings. Buffett started by buying one stock at the age of 11. Those bodybuilders started with one hour a day in the gym. Discipline must be built. It's like body or wealth building. You don't get it by wishing for it. You develop it.

- Maybe you can't create a budget today. But you can save all your receipts and put them in an envelope for a month.
- Maybe you can't save $100 a month, but you can put $1 a day into a jar, or empty your change each day into a jar and then put that into a savings account.
- Maybe you can't wrap your head around everything you're learning about money, but you can ask yourself that one simple question before you buy anything from a fast food meal, to a new music or film CD, to a new outfit or shoes, or tool — "Will buying this _____ make me richer or poorer?" You can still buy it if you must, but by simply asking the question, you're developing discipline.

Some of you are going to develop discipline fast. You're used to and have some discipline already. Others? It's going to take longer. That's how it is. What matters is that you start. As a runner friend of mine who coaches people who want to run a 10K (about five miles), "No matter what kind of shape you're in, or whether or not you can walk 100 yards, you're still ahead of the guy/gal still sitting on the couch wishing they were running."

Everyone learns to develop discipline. Everyone. If you've ever watched a baby learn to walk you notice they fall down a lot. Like, all the time. Then suddenly they don't. They walk more than they fall. Then suddenly they're running. Yes, they fall, but one day they're zipping from one end of the room to the other, and in a few years they're on their school's track team, or racing up and down a basketball court or football field. They didn't start out on the track team. They started out learning to stand up, to take a step, then another. They developed the discipline to keep trying because they wanted to walk, run, and win more than they wanted to sit on a diapered butt and wait to be waited on. It's your choice. Start small. Build that discipline.

- Find an app to remind you to save or track expenses.
- Make a list of financial goals and review them daily.
- Be patient. Discipline takes time.
- Take a class — either Dave Ramsey's Financial Peace University, or something your local community college or bank offers.
- Find someone who can encourage you and hold you accountable to yourself.
- Resist peer pressure—stop hanging around people and places that tempt you to spend or not be financially responsible.
- Make a financial plan and have consequences (like promising to donate $100 to a charity if you don't follow the plan) for not following the plan.
- Create a budget or spending plan.
- Hire a financial coach for a month. It takes 30-40 days to create a new habit and the investment is well worth the cost.

CHAPTER THREE
ARE YOU IN CONTROL OF YOUR FINANCES?
DISCIPLINE, PARKINSON'S LAW, AND LIFE

"It's not how much money you make, but how much money you keep."
~ Robert Kiyosaki

I was enjoying a drink after a round of golf last summer when I over-heard a conversation at a table next to me. It was a father bragging about his youngest son making his "first million." The son was apparently in his mid-20s and a new attorney with a major law firm. A Harvard Law School graduate, he'd gotten a huge signing bonus when he joined the firm, then another bonus when his team won a major case he'd been assigned to.

He was feeling pretty much on top of the world with his quick successes. He had told his father he was looking at $100,000 cars for he and his wife, and a "much deserved" vacation to Greece the following month. The friend the father was telling this story to joked, "I guess he can retire and move onto that yacht now." I laughed to myself. I didn't know anything about this young man, or his life, job or finances but I knew one thing. A million dollars doesn't buy you what it used to. I also knew, as he would likely learn at some point, that "income" does not equal "wealth." They're two very distinct and separate things. If you pursue one without tending to the other you won't have money for long.

I've known or seen far too many millionaires lose their fortunes (income) overnight. I have also counseled many people making six-figure incomes who lived paycheck to paycheck. Judging by the talk of cars and vacations I guessed it would take this young man about six-to-eight months to burn through his first million. Once you buy a couple of $100,000 cars and the insurance you'll need for them, or you take several $20,000 vacations, put down a deposit on a new house and furnishings, and then maintain that lifestyle, you've pretty much tapped all that money (income) out and you'll need to replenish it. You'll have to keep making that much, or more just to keep up.

Congratulations! (Or maybe not) if you live to spend rather than spend to live. If that's the case, you've just joined the ranks of millions of Americans living paycheck-to-paycheck because you don't understand the difference between income and wealth. If paycheck-to-paycheck sounds like something someone making minimum wage does, think again.

"A 2015 Nielsen study, for instance, found 25% of American families making $150,000 or more a year live paycheck to paycheck. One in three households earning between $50,000 and $100,000 find themselves in the same predicament. A higher-income doesn't always translate into financial security."[16]

The amount of money you have earned doesn't tell me how much control you have over your finances or how financially savvy you are. It tells me how well you can make money, not how well you manage it (wealth). As I said, I have taken on many clients making six-figure incomes who were literally living paycheck to paycheck before they came to me. If you make $30,000 a year (the median personal income in the US) or $76,000 a year, (the median family income) you may find it impossible to believe that someone cannot live on $100,000 or more a year.

---

[16] https://www.investopedia.com/articles/personal-finance/091015/why-high-earners-still-live-paychecktopaycheck.asp

How is that possible? It's simple. As our income grows, so do our wants, needs, demands, and standard of living. It's called "Parkinson's Law." More on that later.

Where you live matters too. For instance, the median rent for a two-bedroom apartment in San Francisco is between $3,100 to $5,200 a month—more than three times as much as the $1,420 for a comparable apartment in Charlottesville, Virginia. A small town in West Virginia or a midwestern state would cost even less. Tennessee and Texas have no state income tax, while California's tax rates range from 1% to 12.3%. It's not just housing that costs more. Everything from car insurance, cars, gas, clothing, food, and entertainment also varies. If you like to take a vacation or two a year, have kids in private schools, sports, or music programs, your money goes out a lot faster than it comes in.

Add contributions to a 401K, a professional student loan repayment (Typically $200,000 or more for doctors), and that six-figure income may feel like minimum wage at times. People love spending money and no matter what they make, they rarely have their finances under control.

The only thing that stays consistent across the United States is how we need to manage our money if we're to be financially successful.

Being rich has little to do with the amount of money we have. It has everything to do with how we control and manage it. If you look at the lives of people who win multiple millions in their state's lottery you'll see I'm right. Lottery winners are more likely to declare bankruptcy within three to five years after winning multiple millions than the average American. And, even when they win millions, most of them burn through their winnings faster than they ever thought possible. In one story I read, social worker Sandra Hayes told a reporter, "I know a lot of people who won the lottery and are broke today." "If you're not disciplined, you will go broke. I don't care how much money you have."

Hayes and 12 of her co-workers split a lottery win of $224 million—more than enough, you'd assume, to keep them happy and wealthy for several generations. And, if managed correctly, it could. And if not?

Well, she's exactly right. If you're not disciplined, don't manage your money well, and aren't in control of your money day-to-day, you can lose it all.

It's not just about personal discipline. Look at professional athletes. They're among the most disciplined people on the planet, but they have no more luck managing their money than the rest of us. In a 2012 ESPN documentary called Broke, it was estimated that 78% of NFL players are out of money in less than two years after leaving the game. Why? Most athletes have never had or seen, let alone managed as much money as they make as a pro until they hit the pros. As college graduates scraping through school on scholarships, suddenly coming into a six or even a seven-figure income is a culture shock.

The minimum annual salary for an NFL player is around $480,000, according to the NFL Players Association), or more if they're stars. Russell Wilson, who, according to Forbes, is currently the NFL's highest paid player, recently signed a record four-year, $140 million contract. These large salaries can trigger spending sprees as these athletes struggle to deal with the emotions and high of having so much money. They actually get a high from buying friends and family members houses, cars, and more. Playing the game of football is the least of their problems. As many of them learn, living life and managing their money will soon take up much more of their time than games and game films.[17]

The inability of professional athletes to manage their finances responsibly is so common it has become a serious concern for the NFL. Bankruptcy, money management, substance abuse, and domestic violence

---

[17] https://www.cnbc.com/2019/02/01/heres-what-the-average-nfl-players-makes-in-a-season.html

have become such predominant issues for current and former pro football players that the NFL has made it a requirement for all rookies to attend a four-day symposium. In addition to orientation, the players get lectures on professional responsibility, personal finance, substance abuse, community engagement, and other off-the-field challenges that they will encounter as a professional athlete.[18]

Athletes in other sports don't fare much better. It doesn't matter if you're world famous, or just another name on the roster. Take for example, Dennis Rodman, age 58. He's one of the most notorious, wildest, most outlandish basketball players to ever wear an NBA uniform. These days he's known more for his colorful hair and tattoos, his habit of wearing a dress off the court, and his relationship with singer Madonna. But, Rodman played on the five-time NBA Champion Chicago Bulls with Michael Jordan and Scottie Pippen. He was a seven-time rebounding champion. He was rich. When he retired from the NBA in 2011, not counting his sponsorships and personal appearances and other things he had going outside of basketball, his career earnings were estimated at about $27 million.

A year after retiring, however, he was rumored to be flat broke. But Rodman, as flamboyant and wild as he was, managed money a lot like many of those I have advised. He was married and divorced three times. He was a father who fell behind on child support payments—something millions of divorced parents understand. He was also house rich (a $8.7 million dollar estate in Malibu) and cash poor. It's safe to say that Rodman didn't have a good financial plan.

Like many people with large disposable incomes, his expensive collections were bleeding him dry. In his case it's reported that he'd spent millions of dollars on a heavy metal record collection. The collection reportedly took up two-thirds of the space in his multi-million-dollar

---

[18] https://www.cnbc.com/2019/02/01/heres-what-the-average-nfl-players-makes-in-a-season.html

mansion. A popular rumor said that he would consider selling one or both kidneys to avoid selling his collection. He wasn't just broke. He could be considered in a state of desperation. He was recently arrested for attempting to steal a 400-pound amethyst crystal and other gear from a yoga studio and is rumored to have some heath issues also.[19]

If you look at the stories and lives of many professional athletes you'll understand why the NFL and other sports organizations are so concerned. Movie stars, actors, actresses, even child actors whose parents manage their money, find themselves broke after a lifetime of making millions. No one is exempt from poor financial practices.

We learn from the mistakes of others, and through our own failures, but we don't learn quickly enough. Even if you have a degree (or two), and lots of real-world experience and success, things can still go horribly, horribly wrong. So, with all the educational resources, financial advisors, and experts out there, why do so many people lose control of their finances?

Just ask best-selling author, entrepreneur, and speaker Mike Michalowicz. By the time he was 35 years old Mike had built and sold two multi-million-dollar companies. Confident that he had the formula to success, he became an angel investor…and proceeded to literally lose his entire fortune—everything. Mike is no dummy. PG Lewis & Associates (PGLA), was his second multi-million-dollar company. It grew to national prominence by 2005, by completing large data forensics projects for historically significant court cases, including the Enron collapse.

In an interview about his fall Mike said, "I thought I had done everything right, and on paper it appeared that I had. I successfully built and sold two businesses, I was living the lavish lifestyle of a successful entrepreneur and even used my "vast" knowledge and wealth to invest in

---

[19] https://www.latimes.com/local/lanow/la-me-ln-dennis-rodman-allegedly-stole-clothing-crystal-20190511-story.html

a dozen other startups. In reality, however, I was constantly struggling for survival." Mike told Jared Lindzon of The Bench, he knew the moment he'd gone too far, but was unwilling to admit it at the time. He had to lose everything to learn the difference between income and wealth.

Mike explains his first business was based on setting up computer systems. His second business was a computer crimes investigation firm. His plan was to build both businesses up as much as he could. Like many business owners, his reasoning was that the bigger the business, the more sales he'd make. The more sales he made, the more profit there would be to take home. Of course businesses have expenses, but he figured, "I'd just sell more stuff."

What he learned was that everything he thought he knew or had learned about business, wasn't right. Although he graduated from Virginia Tech with two degrees, one in finance and one in management science, it's his real-world experience with money and entrepreneurship that he writes about in his books. That real-world experience is about becoming savvy about money, and that includes budgeting or creating a spending plan, and practicing discipline.

DISCIPLINE

Many people, including many of my own clients, think there's some sort of special knowledge or skill set that wealthy people have that they don't. I tell them the same thing I'm telling you: It's not rocket science, magic, or special skill sets or smarts. It's financial discipline and education. It's knowing how to manage, save, and invest your money, and how to make it work for you, and then having the discipline to follow through with your financial plan.

"How much you earn has almost no bearing on whether or not you can and will build wealth," financial master David Bach writes. "Regardless of the size of your paycheck, you probably already make enough money to become rich."

Just because a salary has a bunch of zeros tacked on the end of it, that doesn't necessarily equate to wealth. I know we're all accustomed to equating big paychecks with wealth and riches, but that's not how wealth works. At the end of the day, big numbers are just numbers. If the cash behind that number isn't managed properly, it can disappear in the blink of an eye.

As Robert Kiyosaki, author of the personal finance classic, *Rich Dad Poor Dad*, and another one of our financial masters emphasizes in his book, "Most people fail to realize that in life, it's not how much money you make. It's how much money you keep."

Bach says at the end of the day the most important discipline you need is the ability to "pay yourself first." He advocates paying yourself the equivalent of at least one hour a day of whatever your income is, and do it automatically and consistently for the rest of your life. Take that income, whether it's $9 an hour, or $900, and move it into the best 401K account you can find.

What's that got to do with financial discipline? The core definition of financial discipline refers to how well you are able to conform your spending and saving to the plans that you have set to achieve your monetary goals. If you don't have some kind of financial discipline, it doesn't matter how much money you have. Remember, it's not the money, it's what you do with it that matters. Warren Buffett recommends, "Do not save what is left after spending; instead spend what is left after saving."

Financial discipline is not a set of rules, regulations, or a punishment. It is not compliance, obedience, or enforcement. Financial discipline is internal, not external. It's a choice. It's a decision. Financial discipline means resisting the temptation to buy something that catches your eye so you can use that money to follow your spending plan. It means being able to delay gratification because you have a larger goal in mind than just a temporary pleasure. Discipline is being able to make decisions based on something other than emotions.

When we get up and go to the gym when we would like to sleep in rather than work out —that's discipline. You don't develop discipline overnight. It comes with time. Like a muscle, it becomes stronger each time you stress it to the point of fatigue and failure. Many people don't know that muscle is built by tearing down existing muscle, forcing it to grow bigger and stronger. Financial discipline is no different. You'll find yourself hurting and feeling the pain of making decisions about your money you'd prefer not to make. That's how you build discipline. Don't worry. It gets easier the more you build your foundation.

Along with financial discipline comes financial education. You may find you have to educate yourself at the same time you're learning to discipline yourself. That's okay. Stick with it. You'll be pleasantly surprised at how quickly you develop both. One of the most important aspects of financial education clients quickly learn about is Parkinson's Law.

PARKINSON'S LAW

English writer C. Northcote Parkinson developed the law many years ago to explain why most people retire poor. His law says that, no matter how much money people earn, they'll tend to spend it all and then some. Their expenses rise in tandem with their earnings, or in Parkinson's words, "expenditures rise to meet income." In other words, as you earn more money, your needs increase and you end up spending more money. That's why when you made minimum wage in college and couldn't make ends meet, you still can't make ends meet when you're making $75,000 or $100,000 or $500,000.

In order to succeed financially, you must find ways to break Parkinson's law when it comes to money. The first rule of Parkinson's Law says: "Financial independence comes from *violating* Parkinson's Law." In other words you'll only begin to accumulate money when you develop the discipline and willpower to resist the urge to spend everything you make. It's a powerful urge, but a destructive one.

LIFE

"Life is tough, and then you die." Have you ever heard that? Many of us have, and many of us have experienced the fact that life is indeed hard. It's harder for many because they were not taught or didn't learn how to manage their money at a young age. They developed a fear and emotional or mental pain around money instead. When we don't face the fear and pain we already have around money, that's what leads to our losing control of our finances, which leads to a harder life.

A harder life can mean not having money to take a vacation or go out to eat, or to pay your monthly bills, or all the way up to losing your house.

"Look at the mortgage crisis and how many families lost their homes— 3.9 million foreclosures. Look at the amount of money—$1.1 trillion— we owe in student loan debt. The amount ($845 billion) we owe in credit card debt. It's pretty clear that adults don't know much about money.

"To help the next generation avoid the mistakes of their elders, and to live financially fit lives, they need to be taught the essentials about money," says Beth Kobliner, author of the New York Times bestseller *Get a Financial Life*. Kobliner told *Forbes* writer Laura Shin in 2013.[20] Not much has changed in almost a decade except the debts people have, have grown. What's scary is the part about adults not knowing much about money. They still don't. If you're reading this you're trying to learn, or you're hoping to help someone else who needs to learn. Either

---

[20] Laura Shin. Forbes. 5 Most Important Money Lessons to Teach Your Kids. October 15, 2013. https://www.forbes.com/sites/laurashin/2013/10/15/the-5-most-important-money-lessons-to-teach-your-kids/#50cc76a76826

way, it goes to show we're a nation ignorant and fearful of the primary thing so many of us are chasing—money.

ACTION ITEMS

Educate Yourself.

- You're already educating yourself if you're reading this book. But don't stop here. Keep reading, keep learning, and start implementing what you're learning. Don't just read. Listen to podcasts. Watch videos talk to other people going through the same process you are. You can find these people in classes, webinars, and on websites about financial education. If you prefer to meet in person, consider attending Dave Ramsey's "Financial Peace University" — held in local schools, churches, or community centers across the country. People meet in a group once a week for nine weeks to learn how to budget, save, and manage their money.

Develop Financial Discipline.

- One of the things I see most with people trying to turn their financial lives around is a lack of discipline around their spending. It sounds simple to say you'll follow a budget, but when faced with the temptation to spend, many people give in, then beat themselves up for doing so, and quit. If you're not used to sitting down every week to look at what you've made, what you've spent, and how your budget is working out, it's a lot like joining a gym. You go for a few weeks and it's all good, but then your lack of discipline kicks in and one day you decide not to go. That turns into two, three, four days and suddenly you're not going at all any more. The same will happen with your money. Finding a group, a friend, or enlisting your spouse or another responsible adult who can hold you accountable, is a great way to develop the discipline to stay on track. If you don't have that kind of friend, make an appointment with your bank once a month, or hire a financial or life coach to help you.

PARKINSON'S LAW

Resolve to break Parkinson's law (i.e. spend less). You do this by:

Setting Clear Boundaries and Goals

- It's not enough to just to vow to "spend less." You need to create and write down clear and specific spending and saving goals.
- Boundaries are limits we set for and on ourselves. There are different kinds of boundaries, but the ones that matter here have to do with your budget. Be very clear about the limits you set, and how you track them.
- Create incentives and rewards for yourself when you hit your goals. It doesn't have to be big, but it must be motivating. Perhaps you can take the afternoon off and watch a movie, work on your hobbies, spend time with friends you don't see much, or play a round of golf.

Slow Down Your Spending

- Force your expenses to increase at a slower rate than your earnings — spend less than you make and save or invest the difference. If you get a raise, or come into some money, or even if you get a second job, don't spend the extra money. Continue to live "beneath your means." (more on this later)
- If you don't have that extra money right now, then institute an immediate financial freeze. Create a budget of your fixed, unavoidable cost each month and determine to limit your expenditures, at least temporarily, to those costs.

- Then, sit down and examine your other expenses including morning coffee, Candy Crush coins, Uber fares, dinner or lunch out, hair care, clothing, gifts; no amount is too small. Carefully examine every expense. If it's too painful, pretend it's a stranger's spending. Then, look for ways to cut back or eliminate that expense. Aim for a minimum of a 10% reduction in your living costs over the next three months. Then, decide to save and invest 50% of any increase you get from earnings from any source (second job, yard sales, any income). Learn to live on the 50% that remains. Don't worry. You'll survive. You were already surviving on what you made. Remember, this is extra. Do this for the rest of your career. It will soon become a habit and you won't feel the pinch but will appreciate the money you're accumulating.

Build Your Willpower

Until you develop enough willpower to resist the powerful urge to spend everything you make, you won't be able to save money and invest wisely. Developing willpower is hard, but not impossible. Millions have done it and you can also. An acquaintance of mine has been clean and sober since college, when he developed a drinking habit that led to alcoholism. He told me that one of the hardest things to give up wasn't the alcohol. It was the friends and situations where he was when he drank or wanted to drink.

Getting away from old routines, habits, and hangouts was his biggest challenge. Sometimes, he said, it was more helpful just to make changes than to focus on willpower. It didn't really matter what changes, just as long as they were different. He stopped playing poker and watching football at his Frat house. He stopped going out to bars and parties on the weekends and instead started going to movies or staying home and having a game night with other sober friends.

Over time he found that when he wasn't around his drinking friends he didn't have the same urge or temptation to drink. He's been clean and sober for almost forty years now. The same tricks that worked for him can work for you. Stop hanging around the people, places, and situations that tempt you to spend or ignore your budget. Stop going to the mall when you're bored, lonely, or depressed. Stop surfing Amazon.com or clicking on Facebook ads.

- **Stop indulging in "retail therapy."** When we get down it can really help to "buy something," or go shopping to find new shoes, tools, a book, or whatever to make us feel good. But those shopping trips can turn into new cars, boats, and motorcycles too! It can get expensive. To counteract this expensive habit, you simply need to find something else that is healthy for you; something that makes you feel good. It might be joining a gym, going for a walk, taking up a sport or hobby that helps create endorphins (feel good hormones) that replace that "high" we get when we spend. One of my clients told me that when she feels the urge to buy something, she moves that amount of money she wants to spend into a savings account instead. She gets a rush watching the money she isn't spending add up.

- **Eliminate temptation.** Change your spending opportunities. If you love going to the mall, or a favorite store, stop. If you're an online shopper, or a late-night QVC or shopping show fan, stop visiting those websites or watching those shows. Don't put temptation in front of you. Only buy things you *need*, not that you want.

- **Pay with cash.** Dave Ramsey is onto something when it comes to getting people to realize what they're spending. It's a whole lot harder to hand over $150 in cash than it is to swipe your credit or debit card. Start shopping with cash and see if that doesn't make a difference in the amount you spend. It's one of the best willpower tools I know.

CHAPTER FOUR
THE FIVE BASICS YOU NEED TO KNOW ABOUT MONEY

"The single biggest difference between financial success and financial failure is how well you manage your money. It's simple: to master money, you must manage money." ~ T. Harv Eker

I'll never forget a story shared at one of the financial conferences I attended. The guest speaker was a financial advisor and life coach who shared a personal story about one of his college friends. The story shared really resonated with me, mainly because in my career I've consulted many who have already amassed large amounts of wealth, but they still manage that wealth mediocre at best. Over time, every best laid plan can get stale or become outdated.

His story began with a strong comment from his friend Phil. "Don't give me 'the talk,'" Phil told me. Phil, was a former college basketball star. He was still in great physical shape 30 years after he left the basketball court, but he thought his finances hadn't fared as well. He sat across from me in my office. His broad shoulders were drooping, his face was sad.

I'd known Phil since college and yet I was a little confused. I thought he'd been very successful over the years. "What talk?" I asked. "The budget talk." He looked down and away from me as he said it. "I already know all that stuff and budgets don't work," he added. "Have you tried it? Can you show me the last budget you put together?" I asked him. He squirmed in his chair like a teenager, not the middle-aged man he was at the time as he slowly replied, "No."

Phil was a successful commercial real estate broker. He didn't manage his own money very often; he had accountants, a wife, and a CPA who did that for him. They told him if he "could afford" something or not, and for the most part he followed their advice. But recently a commercial property had come up that he really wanted to buy. But, his financial advisors had told him he "couldn't afford it."

"I just closed a deal on a three-million-dollar home yesterday!" he told me. "I can't be broke, but they're (his accountants) are telling me I am!"

Phil wasn't ready to accept their advice. He had come to me to find out what he could and couldn't afford, and to really dig into the numbers. He wanted that property and was willing to do whatever it took to buy it. I asked a few more questions about other investments and then asked to see his bank statements and other papers.

He handed over a portable file folder of documents and a thumb drive. As he did so he finally admitted that he always felt budgets were constricting. They reminded him of his father, a risk averse banker who was always stressing how Phil needed to save his money and pinch pennies.

"I make good money, pay my bills, I deserve to be able to spend my money on what I want to spend it on," Phil said. "Budgets are just too restrictive."

I nodded and he relaxed. Knowing Phil as I do, I changed the subject. I asked him about his business, and how things were going. Knowing he loves to sail I asked him if he'd bought a boat yet.

"No," he laughed. "They're money pits. I'm doing fine renting one when I need it. See?" he said. "I'm not a spendthrift. I didn't buy a $100,000 boat, or the dirt bikes my son wanted. I didn't need a budget to tell me that."

We continued our conversation for a few more minutes, with his telling me about other opportunities he'd turned down, and other money he hadn't spent. I flipped through the papers he'd handed me and pulled up his bank records from the thumb drive.

In Phil's mind he'd been financially responsible. As I looked through his statements, I saw a different story. As he talked, I started taking notes on what I was seeing and hearing.

"I'm just waiting," he said. "I'll know it when I see it. You have to say no to 100 opportunities so you can say yes to the one you really want." I nodded again.

"Budgets are like that too," I said. "What do you mean?" he asked. I put my pen down and looked up at him. "Budgets are just a way of saying no to the things you don't really need so you ensure you have enough money to buy the things you really want," I said.

The look on his face was priceless. "I don't understand," he said. I lifted up the stack of papers and pointed to the dinners out, the money he'd spent on flying first class, his wine collection, and the vacations he'd taken. I tallied up the numbers. "If you flew business class, took one or even two vacations a year instead of a week-long vacation every other month, and limited your wine purchases to a dozen bottles a month instead of a few dozen cases a month, you'd have had half of the down payment you need for this building," I said, handing him my notes.

While he looked at my notes, I kept going through his bank statements and found enough money on other purchases (dinner parties, memberships, etc.) and pointed out that he could make his monthly mortgage on the building by sacrificing certain items, and by selling his $150,000 car and buying a more modest $50,000 one.

"How did you do that?" he asked. "I created a quick and dirty budget based on what I saw in your bank statements," I replied. "If you had had a budget you'd be able to sit down and see what you're spending your money on and where you could cut back even more. True, you didn't make large purchases, like boats and dirt bikes, but you also didn't see how much a few $100 dinners, and $300 cases of wine, and that gym membership no one uses, and all those expenses really cost you. A hundred dollars here and there adds up."

We spent the rest of the afternoon and into the evening going over his financials. By the time we were done Phil finally understood that a budget would free him up to get what he wanted, not keep him from enjoying his success or the money he made.

His advisors had done their job by trying to keep up with what they thought Phil wanted, but not with what would have best served Phil. They were merely moving money around to ensure he could keep his lifestyle. They hadn't confronted him on how he was spending his money.

Once Phil understood a budget was about choices, not restrictions, he dove headlong into creating a spending plan that would give him the financial security to get what he really wanted. I'd like to be able to say he was able to buy the property he wanted, but he didn't. He did find something he liked almost as much, and closer to the water he liked being around. Like most of us who start a budget, there was a learning curve and it took time for him, and his kids, to get good at following a budget. It was rough, but ultimately everyone realized after the initial change, life was better on a budget.

Many of my clients are initially like Phil. They hear the word "budget" and immediately recoil, feeling a budget will deny them the things they've worked so hard to earn and that they feel they deserve. That's why I refer to budgets now as "spending plans." A spending plan implies a direct purpose and plan for your money to take. It's about the financial goals you want to achieve. A spending plan is a little more active and directed, while a budget is more about cutting things out, and denying yourself things you want or think you deserve.

Paula Pant, host of the "Afford Anything" podcast on financial freedom says it best, "You can afford anything but not everything. Every choice is a trade-off against something else. Saying yes to one thing implicitly means saying no to something else, and that doesn't just apply to your money. It applies to your time, your energy, your focus, your attention, anything in your life that's a scarce or limited resource. And so the questions become twofold. Number one, what's most important to you? What do you truly value? And number two, how do you make daily decisions accordingly? How do your day-to-day actions reflect what you value the most?"[21]

These are the questions I ask you. When you wake up to the reality we all only have 24 hours in a day, then having financial, personal, business, and relationship boundaries becomes your greatest superpower. Do you want to make more money, or spend more time with family and friends?

Jay Leno owns 286 vehicles—169 cars and 117 motorbikes. Even if he only spent a few minutes a day on every one, he wouldn't be able to drive them all in a week. He must decide which vehicle to ride or drive and say "no," to one so he can enjoy another. Phil could afford anything he wanted, but not everything he wanted. Life is all about choices, but you can't make smart choices until you have control of your money, manage it well, and have clearly stated and written goals for it. That means becoming educated about your money.

Once you start reading, researching and thinking about money you'll start to see there's a lot of information, but that it all boils down to a few basics. There are probably about a dozen basics, but I'm going to give you my top five because they're the ones most clients find helpful.

---

[21] Paula Pant. AffordAnything.com. https://affordanything.com/about/

THE FIVE BASICS YOU NEED TO KNOW ABOUT MONEY:

"If you do what you've always done, you'll get what you've always gotten." ~ Tony Robbins

ONE: GET CONTROL OF YOUR MONEY — CREATE A SPENDING PLAN AND SAVE, SAVE, SAVE

"When you fix your finances you fix your life." David Bach told entrepreneur and interviewer Marie Forleo on her show.[22] The two were discussing Bach's book, *The Latte Factor, Why You Don't Have to Be Rich, to Live Rich.* It seems obvious, but to millions of people it's not. Too many people spend and save "on the fly," or "by the seat of their pants." They guess at their bank balance. They keep an estimated balance in their heads—"I think I've got $150 in the bank. I can afford this." They think they have control over their money, but they don't.

They haven't taken the time to create a budget or spending plan, or to balance their checkbook, or to set financial goals they actually track. Bach's right. When you fix your finances, meaning you get control over your money, and you give every dollar a job, you'll be amazed at how not only your money, but your life turns around.

"Here's the truth: Debt is debt. Probably the most important lesson of the recession is that the only difference between good debts and bad debts is that the bad variety can destroy your financial life more quickly. . . I believe that in today's economy, getting out of debt fast is the most important financial move you and your family can make. The faster you are debt free, the faster you are really free," Bach says.[23]

This seems obvious, but you'd be surprised by how many people want to start investing, buying, spending, or making decisions about their

---

[22] https://www.marieforleo.com/2019/05/david-bach-latte-factor/
[23] http://www.oprah.com/money/david-bach-how-to-avoid-making-personal-finance-mistakes_1/all#ixzz644QZu8Gu

money before it's under their control. Psychologists tell me it's a form of avoidance or denial. As long as they're doing "something," they feel like they're in control, even when they're not. When things don't work out and they fail, they're devastated. It's like business—being busy doesn't necessarily mean you're being productive.

So my number one tip is to get control of your money. That means setting up a budget. I prefer calling it your "Spending Plan" that will work for you and one that you will follow. Setting up a budget is easy. Following it, updating it, and making the adjustments you need to stay in control is the hard part. Before you start investing anything you should have at least six months of expenses saved in an emergency fund. Preferably more if you can. Once you're comfortable with your new spending plan, you're ready to invest and do more with your money.

Most financial experts, including myself, are fans of some form of what Dave Ramsey calls "The Debt Snowball Plan." It involves saving up $1,000 for your emergency fund, then listing all your debts, from highest to lowest interest rates, and highest to lowest debt. You pay the minimum on each debt, and the maximum on the lowest debt until it is paid off. Then, Ramsey says, you roll over what you were paying on the lowest debt onto the next highest debt. Continue doing this until all your debts are paid off. It's that simple. It's not easy, but it is simple. The most important thing this does is begin to give you control over your money. The debt snowball is part of a larger plan, but paying off those debts each month and seeing them get smaller and smaller, is highly motivating when it comes to managing your money and your debt.

I can't stress this enough. Not being in control of your money is like getting on the road without having properly maintained your car. It's entirely possible that nothing can happen for years, lulling you into a false sense of security, but ultimately the worst *will* happen when your failure to maintain your vehicle results in an accident, or failure, or worse.

Creating a "Spending Plan" means more than just tracking money in and money out. It also includes understanding where your money comes from, where it goes, and what it is doing, or not doing for you. This means you need to have a system for:

- Paying yourself first
- Debt and credit management through budgeting
- Saving as a lifestyle
- Tracking and growing your income
- Giving your money (every dollar!) a job to do
- Paying bills on time to improve your credit
- Thinking about retirement — even if you're only 20 years old!

How do you get started? Simple:

TWO: EDUCATE YOURSELF AND UNDERSTAND HOW YOUR MONEY WORKS

I struck up a lengthy conversation with a man on a plane after he learned I was a financial advisor. He told me his teenage son had made enough money for a down payment on a new car in only six months. The boy was only 14 years old.

"Next year he'll be able to afford a better car than the one I'm driving," he laughed.

I was intrigued. "How is he making his money?" I asked. "Clocks," he replied. "You know, like clocks on your car's dashboard, your oven, wherever. He charges people $5 to set their clocks. $5 for one, $10 for up to five others. It's worth it to a lot of people," he said. "But he goes the extra mile and types up the instructions for them. They tell him what they have, he finds it online, and gives them the instructions after he sets the clock. Not all of us can read instructions, or some people lose the instructions or don't understand what they say."

I thought about it. I'd pay $5 to have my car clocks set to the right time and have someone show me how to do myself. "That's a lot of clocks," I said. "Oh, it's not just clocks," the man said. "He's a friendly kid and people like him. He started doing this to buy a skateboard. He asked me what he could do to make money in addition to his allowance. I asked him what skills he had. That's what he came up with. He had set all the clocks in our house and loved doing it. What the heck? We made some flyers and he handed them out or put them in people's mailboxes. He got some calls, word about him got around on Facebook and boom. Suddenly he's got an income. He bought his skateboard, then started thinking about buying a car, and set some bigger goals for himself, like college.

"Anyway, with the clocks, it just escalated. Once he's in people's homes fixing their clocks and chatting, they ask him what else he does. He ends up mowing lawns, raking leaves, walking their dog, and pet sitting when they go out of town. He's cleaned out garages, attics, basements, or done whatever odd jobs they have. He's dependable and does a good job, so people are always hiring him for things. He made more money last weekend than I make in a week. I might have to ask him for a job!"

We talked about saving, goals, and how his son was learning to manage the money he was making. Apparently, he was taking a class at school that taught students the basics on how to budget, save, and invest. When he opened a bank account as part of the class, he got to talking to the banker. He learned about a free online course the bank offered in money management for its customers. He took that online class but craved more. From his online research about making and managing money he started reading about how to become an entrepreneur, how to do sales, how to provide customer service and so on.

"Something just clicked with him I guess. He's really excited about what he's doing," the man said. "He's not into sports or music or anything, but numbers, math, people — the perfect storm. I have an entrepreneur on my hands now. That's a good thing! He got me to thinking about money and we started learning together about investing and the stock market. That's his next adventure. He'd have loved to meet you," he said. "He'd exhaust you with questions, but he'd love it."

We laughed, but it got me thinking too. "Educating" yourself about money doesn't just mean learning how to make and save and budget money. This kid understood that the more he learned about all kinds of things having to do with money — how to manage it, how to make it, how to use it, how to leverage it, the more of it he would have. I gave the man some tips and a list of books to read on investing, and hopefully helped him with his son. What a great example of how parents and kids, or any family members, can learn from and with each other.

Money apparently didn't scare this kid, but it does scare a lot of us. We're so caught up in the emotional aspects of money we're frozen. We're so conflicted about whether money and wealth is a good thing or a bad thing, or what having it or not having it says about us as people that we tend to forget that money is just a tool.

How well we learn to use that tool depends on how much we can do with it. Experts tell me that children as young as three years old can understand money. Maybe your toddlers can't understand more complex aspects of money, but they totally understand that money buys them toys and food they want. When given a choice between a nickel and a dime they'll always choose the nickel because it's bigger.

While children don't immediately grasp the value of money they do understand it's important. Start young though. A study by the University of Cambridge found that money habits in children are formed by the time they're seven years old.[24] That doesn't mean we can't change our

---

[24] https://mascdn.azureedge.net/cms/the-money-advice-service-habit-formation-and-learning-in-young-children-may2013.pdf

financial habits when we're older, just that it's harder once they've become ingrained in us. The earlier we learn, the better our financial future.

Dave Ramsey has some great tips on teaching kids about money. He doesn't like the word "allowance," so he uses the word "commission." He explains that when you work, you get paid—a commission, just like the real world. "Work. You must work. For kids, eating two bags of Doritos and spending all day in a chair playing Nintendo is not work," he says. "Work, get paid. Don't work. Don't get paid. It's a very simple concept!"[25]

Years ago a client of mine received several power tools from his wife's family. They assumed he, like most of the men in his wife's family, was interested in woodworking. Unfortunately, at the time, he was doing well to know which end of a screwdriver to hold. Suddenly he had a garage with several thousand dollars' worth of tools he knew nothing about. He was not only clueless about them, but they scared him. The noise, safety concerns, the complexity of operating them all intimidated him. But, he feared his wife's family's disapproval more than he feared the tools. The idea of them pitying him for not being a woodworker inspired him to at least learn how to use the table saw and planer they'd given him.

So he hired a local carpenter to teach him how to use the tools safely and how to do basic things like building boxes and making toys. From there he graduated into finding local projects for neighbors that he could tackle by himself. At first, he didn't think he'd like woodworking, he told me. But once he understood how to use the tools he fell in love with it. Over the years he added to his tool shop now relocated in the upstairs of his barn. When I was invited to see the "Shop Makeover" I was very impressed. This individual added to his initial gift by adding every wood

---

[25] https://www.daveramsey.com/askdave/relationships-and-money/teaching-kids-four-money-principles

tool making machine possible, and could now make practically anything from scratch including cabinets, chests and novelty items.

It is truly amazing what a little education and initiative can bring out in a person.

Money, as I said, is also a tool. It can be intimidating, scary, and feel like it's more power than we could ever handle. Like my client and his tools, by starting with small things, getting more experienced people to teach us the basics, we build up to bigger projects as we become more proficient. My neighbor was happy just learning how to use the table saw. But months later that small skill turned into his making cabinets and furniture. The teenager I described didn't start off wondering about investing. He learned about budgeting and saving, and wants and needs and how to build his credit. Then he turned to investing.

If I could only tell people one thing about money it would be that it's a very versatile tool and one they should learn to master by learning about it and understanding what it can do, then getting out there and implementing what they've learned. Yes, you may struggle initially but that's how we learn.

When people stop feeling guilty for having money, or not having money, for spending it, or wishing they had more to spend, or for failing to manage it as well as they like, they begin to take control of their money, not fear it. Money literally does become a tool—one they can then use to achieve their goals, to make their dreams come true, to use to help themselves and the ones they love.

Start small but start. Get control of, then master your money.

THREE: REMEMBER PARKINSON'S LAW: LIVE WITHIN OR UNDER YOUR MEANS

When you've lived in a small apartment most of your adult life and you've just scraped to get by, it makes sense to move into something bigger and better when you start making money. But that doesn't mean to stretch your budget to the max to get the biggest place you can afford!

Warren Buffet, the man who could buy any property anywhere in the world, lives in a modest house that's worth .001% of his total wealth. The house is located in a quiet neighborhood of Omaha, Nebraska. He bought the house for $31,500 in 1958 or about $250,000 in today's dollars. It's now worth an estimated $652,619. Not exactly what you'd think he would own is it? He calls it the "third-best investment he's ever made." It's 6,570 sq. feet and has five bedrooms and 2.5 bathrooms. Fences and security cameras guard the property. Why hasn't he moved to a more extravagant home? He told BBC, "I'm happy there. I'd move if I thought I'd be happier someplace else."

It's not the only real estate Buffett owns. He recently sold his Laguna Beach, California, home for about $7.5 million, according to representatives of Villa Real Estate. The home comes with a $9,264 annual association fee. It was a beach retreat for his family, but he found he wasn't using the house much since his first wife died, so he sold it. If you're not using something, be it a lawnmower, car, or above ground swimming pool or trampoline, get rid of it. Maintenance costs are costing you money every day! Sell it. Put the money you were spending into savings or invest it.

Maybe worrying about which million-dollar property to buy or what continent to live on isn't a problem you have yet. Maybe doing something like never buying a cup of coffee and saving the cost of that cup is where you are. Sound crazy? Don't laugh.

Multimillionaire Suze Orman says she will "never buy a cup of coffee anywhere." In fact, she repeatedly tells people, "You are peeing $1 million down the drain as you are drinking that coffee. Do you really want to do that? No." She explained to CNBC in a 2019 interview that $100 a month—a little more than $3 on coffee a day—would turn into $1 million after 40 years in a Roth IRA. That's assuming a healthy 12%

return, but even at 7%, that'd give you an extra $250,000 for your golden years. Does that sound so crazy after all?[26]

According to a 2017 survey from the investment app Acorns, almost half (45%) of younger millennials put more money toward coffee than their retirement savings!

If merely saving $100 a month on coffee can reap so many rewards, think about one of the larger expenses millions of us have that we could turn into savings if we simply sold, trashed, or got rid of our "stuff." It never ceases to amaze me how much money people spend on storage units.

According to Marcus & Millichap, an investment real estate company that tracks the self-storage industry, this year, the average national monthly cost of a climate-controlled rental space is expected to reach $1.63 per square foot. Translation? You could spend nearly $2,000 in one year for the most popular 10' x 10' unit. In higher cost areas, their storage costs are even higher. Typically, prices for that space rises to $2,500 (in Los Angeles) to more than $3,700 (in New York City).

When you think about what people store in their units, it's easy to see that most of us could buy whatever's in there when we need it instead of storing it and then trying to find it. Most people don't know what they have in their units, and most couldn't find it if they needed to. There are countless stories of people owning duplicates and even triplicates of items because they've simply forgotten it's there.

"It's typically all about procrastination," says Ann Gambrell. Gambrell is a founder of the National Association of Professional Organizers. The association runs decluttering workshops and clutter support groups around the country. Gambrell told Consumer Reports writer Carla Fried, "People end up spending money because they can't make a decision."

---

[26] https://www.marketwatch.com/story/suze-orman-wants-you-to-stop-peeing-1-million-down-the-drain-2019-03-28

Okay, some of us do use storage units wisely. Instead of incurring another $1,000 to $2,000 for a bigger apartment in New York City, it makes sense to have a $300 storage unit for your stuff—if you're using the stuff you're storing. Or, if you're in the midst of buying or selling a home, a temporary storage unit in the interim makes sense. The key word is "temporary." If you add up the costs and weigh the benefits of the unit against what you're spending for it, you can decide for yourself if you're making a smart decision. Most people aren't.

According to the Self-Storage Association, more than half of self-storage renters keep a unit for a year or more. Is what you're storing worth the $4,000 to $6,000 you're paying to 'store your stuff'? One of the best pieces of advice I've heard comes from a Facebook group called Organizing Advice for Clutter bugs, run by three-time bestselling author and professional organizer Cassandra Aarssen.

One of her group members recently posted:

"I sold everything in my two 10x15 storage units and put the money I made, about $1,500, in a savings account. I now put the $350 I was spending renting the units each month into that same account. When I find I need something that I once had in my units, I take money out of that account and go buy whatever it is I've needed. So far (one year), I've spent $45. I now have enough money for a down payment on a used car ($3,600)."

When you start looking at what your money does, and what its job is, you'll start looking differently at what you spend your money on. That $3,600 invested into the right stocks or mutual funds could become enough to outright purchase a brand-new car in a few years — although a nearly new used car would be a better investment.

This holds true for all our habits. How much do you spend on tobacco, alcohol, dinner out, soda, coffee, treats for your pets, bottled water versus a water filter in your home?

Even if you get a great deal on a lawnmower, do you use it? How much is the mower, maintenance, repairs compared with hiring someone to mow your lawn for you when it's needed?

When you start looking at things with what their true cost is, not just how much you paid for them, things change.

FOUR: SAVE, SAVE, SAVE: It's been decades since I've heard the old story about the ants and the grasshopper. Remember that childhood story? The ants work hard all summer to lay up seeds and grass and food for the winter. The grasshopper, on the other hand, plays all summer, making music on his violin, and dancing the days away. He laughs at the ants working and toiling in the hot sun until late autumn comes, and he can find no food. He goes to the ants and asks for some of their grain. "I danced and made music all summer and had no time to lay up food," he tells them. The ants are disgusted with him and his lack of saving. "Then dance and play," they tell him. "We have no food for you."

Even if you are only able to save $1 a week, save it. If you can, have a yard sale, get a second or third job. Give up buying coffee or eating out, and save that money, it will add up. Dave Ramsey's followers have some amazing stories about "finding" ways to pay off ten, twenty, thirty or even fifty thousand dollars in debt over a few years. Many get a second or third job, from delivering pizzas, starting a small business online, or taking up couponing. Some give up gym memberships and dining out. What amazes people is how much even small things, like buying a soda, tea, or a cup of coffee a day can cost over a year. And if you put those dollars into a compounding account, they also add up there as well!

Many of us have heard of Dale Carnegie. For those of you who haven't, Carnegie was an American writer and lecturer and author of the bestselling book *How to Win Friends and Influence People*. He developed some very famous courses in self-improvement, salesmanship, corporate training, public speaking, and interpersonal skills. Born into poverty, Carnegie turned his pennies and dollars into a fortune. It can be done. It takes discipline, understanding how your money works, goals, a spending plan, and time to make it happen. Start now. You'll see your money begin to accumulate significantly in months.

FIVE: DON'T FORGET BASIC'S 1-4

SIX STEPS TO FINANCIAL SUCCESS

Every expert has their own set of favorite "steps to success." Learn them all and use what works for you. I particularly like Napoleon Hill's favorite steps. If you're familiar with "SMART goals" you will recognize these:

STEP ONE: You must have a specific goal. Hill was making $10,700 a year as Athletic Director and Head Football Coach. He thought about his goal long and hard, and eventually decided he wanted an income of $30,000 a year, guaranteed for life.

STEP TWO: You must have a specific time to achieve your goal. At the age of 28, Hill gave himself 10 years to reach his goal, vowing to be financially independent by the age of 38.

STEP THREE: You must write your goal(s) down. Your goal must be specific, and you must write it down as a commitment. It doesn't have to be anything fancy. Hill wrote down his goal on a piece of cardboard and placed it on his daily calendar.

STEP FOUR: You must develop a plan to achieve your goal. Hill had saved $40,000 in two and a half years working part-time. He decided if he committed his $40,000 for 10 years and could get 10% interest, his savings would be $40,000 x 10% x 10 years = $100,000. (Actually, he said, the $40,000 would grow to more than $100,000, but he wanted his plan to be easy to understand). Hill figured that if he accumulated $300,000 cash, and received 10% interest, he could withdraw $30,000 each year and never touch my principal. This $30,000 could go on for-ever. But he needed $300,000 and he had only figured out how to get $100,000 by investing the $40,000 he had saved.

He was still $200,000 short. he figured that at 10% interest he would have to save $1,000 a month for 10 years to get the additional $200,000; $1,000/month at 10% interest = $200,000 plus. He now had his final plan. Invest his $40,000 for 10 years and invest $1,000 per month for 10 years. $300,000 would equal $30,000 a year for life.

STEP FIVE: You must decide what kind of price you are willing to pay to reach your goal. Saving $1,000 a month was tough for Hill, but he knew that if he wanted to be totally financially independent in 10 years, that was what it would take. "There is no free lunch."

STEP SIX: You must think about reaching your goal every day. There was not one day Hill says he didn't think about how great being totally financially independent would be. Those dreams made him keep trying when he wanted to quit.[27]

Dave Ramsey has a great saying, "Live like no one else now, so later you can live like no one else." What he means is that if you're willing to make some sacrifices, and live like no one else now, while you pay off your debt, later, when you're debt free you can live like no one else (in debt) is living.

GIVING YOUR MONEY A JOB

When you start setting up a budget, one of the things you need to realize is that every dollar you make should have a job. This is where calling your budget your "spending plan," makes more sense. By "job" I mean a purpose. When every dollar has a job you know exactly where your income is going and it's going exactly where you want it to go. That means your money is doing what you designed it to do in your budget

---

[27] https://www.influencive.com/think-grow-rich-six-steps-true-success/

or spending plan. It also eliminates guilt. If, for instance, you have $100 per month for "entertainment/movies," then you can enjoy spending that $100 without feeling guilty for spending money you should spend on rent or utilities on going out for dinner or watching a movie.

Ideally you should budget every dollar you have coming into a category until you reach $zero. Some people prefer to leave an amount of money unassigned each month in case they run out of money in a category. We call this category "Available to Budget," so it really does have a job. Having an "Available to Budget" category isn't necessary if you budget wisely and adjust your budget so it's more realistic each week or month.

If you do have money left over, you can funnel your dollars into another job—for expected and unexpected emergencies, for instance. Let's say you know your car is going to need tires, or your furnace is making funny noises that mean a repairman is in your future. You may have just found water in the basement, or water stains on the ceiling and you know you're going to need either repairs or a new roof. You know you're going to get socked with an expensive emergency, but you don't know which is going to come first, or when it's coming, or if it will be followed by another emergency, but you're expecting it. What you might not foresee are health issues, a car accident that leaves you unable to work, an unplanned pregnancy, or the death or illness of a loved one.

Expected and unexpected emergency funds are called your "Rainy Day fund," or simply an "Emergency Fund." They shouldn't be used for anything except for true emergencies. Dave Ramsey encourages people to have a minimum of $1,000 in their rainy-day fund but suggests working towards having 3-to-6 months' worth of personal expenses in the fund. So, whether your monthly expenses are $2,000 or $20,000 ultimately you should have up to six months of expenses in a savings account, or someplace where you can access it quickly.

FINANCIAL DISCIPLINE — WHAT IT IS, HOW TO DEVELOP IT

When Daymond Johns business, FUBU took off, he said he experienced a huge financial windfall and wasn't quite prepared for it. (FUBU is an American hip hop apparel company. FUBU stands for "For Us, By Us.") All of us have at one time come into money, expectedly or not. We get a bout of what my southern friends call "redneck rich." We get ahead and suddenly we have an urge to spend that excess, or a lot of it. And just as quickly as it came, it's gone. Daymond Johns and other financial gurus aren't immune to this. None of us are.

Daymond John began his career selling $10 hats outside the New York Coliseum. Now, he's worth $250 million. Who wouldn't be tempted to buy whatever they wanted? When FUBU started producing he went from struggling financially to suddenly having more money than he could spend, although he tried.

"I purchased a couple of homes," he told reporter Mike Foss of FTW. "I remember when I went down to Miami shopping and I ended up buying two homes. It wasn't too bright, but that's what I did."

Mike Michalowicz bought cars, expensive cars. One for his wife, one for him, and he said he remembers standing in the showroom and saying, "I have more money than God," and feeling something break inside. He knew something had happened, but it wasn't until later when he lost everything that he knew he didn't really.

INVESTING 101

It's never too soon to talk about investing, even if you don't have five dollars to invest right now. It's important to be learning about investing, and to be setting investment goals, so when you do have a few dollars, you're ready. Here are the basics of investing:

- **What does investing mean?** According to Investopedia.com, "an investment is an asset or item acquired with the goal of generating income or appreciation. In an economic sense, an investment is the purchase of goods that are not consumed today but are used in the future to create wealth. In finance, an investment is a monetary asset purchased with the idea that the asset will provide income in the future or will later be sold at a higher price for a profit."[28]

- **Understand what investing means, and what you're investing in before you part with one dollar of your hard-earned savings.** Once you start saving money, you'll hear more and more from those who know you're saving, about where should invest it. Ignore the pressure to invest until you understand what you're doing. There's no risk in keeping your money in a savings account until you do understand the basics of investing. It's better to delay any returns than lose everything you've saved by making a poor investment.

- **Investing can take a lifetime to learn, so there's no rush.** Even Warren Buffett doesn't have the science and art down pat yet, and he's been investing for over half a century. He still makes mistakes. This isn't something you're going to nail the first time out. So, don't feel intimidated by it. You might find you have a knack for it, but it doesn't mean you're infallible. No one is.

- **Saving and investing are two different things.** Saving is accumulating money (think piggy bank) and investing makes your money multiply over time. The big difference is the time and the type of account you use to hold your money. Saving is for short-term goals; investing is for medium term, long term and retirement goals.

- **There are several ways to invest: Individual stocks, Individual bonds, bond mutual funds, closed end mutual funds, index mutual funds, and ETFs (exchange-traded funds).** Learn

---

[28] https://www.investopedia.com/terms/i/investment.asp

as much as you can about each one and understand how each one can impact you and your goals. Each investment type has its pros and cons. If you're not sure you understand the pros and cons, that's okay. A financial advisor can suggest the best investment for you based on your goals, the amount you have to invest, and other criteria.

CHOOSING A FINANCIAL ADVISOR, QUESTIONS TO ASK

What is a financial advisor? A financial advisor is a money management professional who helps you save or invest for your specific financial goals. Financial advisors can also assist with tax planning, estate planning or insurance coverage.

There are many reasons why people consider hiring a financial planner. Here are just a few:

- They feel lost, confused, or uncertain about how to plan their financial future. They need solid, practical advice and a good roadmap.
- They are not "money people." Money scares, intimidates, or confuses them They just don't want to deal with it. They're more comfortable hiring a professional who will deal with it for them.
- They enjoy managing their money but want that added edge and insight a professional can offer. Or, they have a lot of decisions to make, but want an impartial third party to weigh in with their opinion. They know that no matter how much they learn about investing, they'll never be a Wall Street pro. And even if they are a Wall Street pro, they know everyone can benefit from an impartial third-party look.

They have come into an inheritance, or a new job with a significantly larger income (think professional athletes, attorneys, doctors, celebrities etc.)

Some people may feel they don't need or aren't ready for a financial advisor. If you think you might be, ask yourself these questions:

- **Where are you in your process of planning your financial future?** Figure out what services you actually need so you don't pay for expertise or services you don't need. Do you just need to get started investing in your financial goals? If so, you may not need a face-to-face human advisor. If you only need investment management, consider a robo-advisor. These computer-based services choose and manage an investment portfolio for you and do so at a low fee. If you have questions, some even offer access to financial advisors. There's usually low to no account minimum so it's easy to get started. Do you have things like estate management or planning, insurance issues, inheritance management etc.? Then you might need more personalized advice.

- **Do you want personalized financial advice, but not a face-to-face sit down?** Online financial planning may cost less than you'd pay a traditional in-personal financial advisor. You meet online, by phone or video chat. The advisor is human, but just not sitting across from you in a sticks and brick office. You'll get complete investment management and holistic financial planning; and you'll have a dedicated advisor or certified financial planner. If you don't have deep pockets and a lot of money to spend, you can often be paired with a team of advisors.

- **Do you have a simple, complex or special circumstances situation?** Depending on your situation's complexity, you may want a local advisor or a wider array of financial expert advice. For example, you may need to explore revocable, irrevocable or special needs trusts. Life insurance trusts, life insurance needs along with health and disability coverages may cause the need for you to retain a local financial advisor or trust attorney.

WHEN SHOULD YOU HIRE A FINANCIAL ADVISOR?

So, you have some money, or are just starting a new job or career where you will have some money. When should you start looking for or considering a financial advisor?

Immediately, when you are ready to get serious about your financial future. You might ask yourself the question, can I afford an advisor at this time of my life? I like to say, "You can't afford not to." If you really want financial independence, a good advisor can truly help improve your financial affairs regardless of your income or assets currently.

Financial advisors do not need to be expensive. And while everyone can benefit from a financial plan, not everyone may need a costly full-blown plan like a multi-millionaire. Most advisors will tailor a plan based on your income, assets & the complexity of your personal situation. Many advisors will also be open to help you focus on fixing one or two immediate concerns like retirement planning, college savings, insurance or elder care planning and charge accordingly.

There are three types of advisors: Fee Only, Commission Only, and a Hybrid Advisor who is registered to offer fee only services as well as commission products.

Fee-only advisors charge a percentage (usually 1%) of the money they invest for you. Let's say you have $200,000 to invest. With that 1% fee you would pay $2,000 a year. If you have a million dollars, the fee will jump to $10,000 a year. Some advisors do have a sliding fee structure in which the percentage they charge drops as your assets increase. I say "$200,000" because the average advisor may not be as willing to talk to you for less than $100,000. Some may drop as low as $10-25,000.00 depending on the RIA's or Broker dealer mandates. Many advisors will work with lower minimums if someone else in your family is utilizing their services as well. They will be more open to working with you on your small account since they already have another family member with a fair amount under management. We call that "house holding" an account. You can also hire an advisor for $1,000 to $2,000 to create a plan for you, or to review an existing plan. Sometimes getting a second opinion makes a lot of sense.

If you're prepared, serious, and able to put a plan into action once you have it, it makes sense to invest in an advisor to look at your plan or create a plan.

QUESTIONS TO ASK YOUR FINANCIAL ADVISOR

According to Investopedia, the top reason people end up firing their financial advisors is not how they perform, but how they communicate, or how they fail to communicate.

"Clients don't necessarily fire advisors only because of poor performance, but instead because the advisor never communicates with them," Bill Hammer, Jr., a principal founder of the Hammer Wealth Group, a Melville, N.Y. wealth management firm told Investopedia in October 2019. Communication is a big issue: miscommunication, not listening to clients, or not communicating with them for long periods of time each can cause a switch. Poor or no communication from your advisor can be more than annoying. It can lead to poor investor behavior, such as buying or selling at the wrong time.

If you pick the wrong advisor, you may get the feeling that your advisor is "asleep at the wheel," or just "phoning in" their performance and not really caring about you or your money at all. If your money isn't performing, many advisors choose to remain silent so they do not draw attention to the problem, but Hammer says that during disappointing periods of performance, it is crucial for advisors to communicate with their clients, even though many pass on that advice and risk losing their clients in the process.[29]

---

[29] https://www.investopedia.com/articles/professionals/071113/why-clients-fire-financial-advisors.asp

Rita Gunther McGrath, an Associate Professor at the Columbia University Business School, didn't hesitate to fire her advisor when she didn't like the numbers and performance she was seeing. This happens a lot— more than it should. But it's mostly, says Investopedia, over communication issues.

If you take time during your interviews and search for a financial advisor, the top criteria you should look at is how well, how often, and how they communicate with you. Having the best financial advisor in the world is useless if they don't communicate with you regularly and take an active role in advising you about your money and your investments. Here are some questions you can start with:

- **What are your qualifications?** This is a standard question, but most people don't know what qualifications, certifications etc. they should be looking for. The alphabet soup of initials and titles can confuse anyone not familiar with the meanings. Start by checking out The Financial Industry Regulatory Authority's professional designations database. They'll list each designation and certification and will tell you what they mean. They'll also tell you if there are any education requirements; who, if anyone, accredits the designation. Most importantly, they'll tell you whether there's a published list of disciplinary actions. You can also check a professional status and see if they actually are who they claim to be.
- **What's your investment philosophy?** Are they high risk while you're low risk? Or vice versa? It's vital to make sure that you have the same investment philosophy. Your advisor needs to believe in what they're doing and stick with it. For instance, when the market is down, and they can convince you to wait it out so you don't sell at the bottom of a cycle because you're scared. They need to be confident and convinced of what they're doing and why they're doing it.

- **How does our relationship work once I hire you?** In other words, how much access will you have to them, and what will it cost? Once you hire your advisor do they disappear, or will you have easy access to them? Can you email, call, text or email them with questions, or will they hand you off to a clerk or associate? How often will you hear from them, and in what form? How often can you schedule appointments?

- **What's my gut say?** Intuition and the feeling that you "like" or "trust" or dislike or distrust an advisor should always be taken into consideration. Trust your gut. It may or may not make sense to you at the time, but if nothing else, back off and give things a chance to play out more before hiring someone you don't feel good about hiring—no matter what their credentials. They may be a good fit for someone else, but not you.

- **Who are your typical clients?** Find an advisor who knows and understands your financial situation and is used to other clients with similar situations. You want them to be able to help you meet *your* goals, not theirs.

- **Who is your custodian?** In light of the Bernie Madoff scam, this is important. Ideally, your financial advisor has an independent custodian, such as a brokerage firm, to hold your investments, rather than act as his or her own custodian. Bernie Madoff was able to defraud clients through his Ponzi scheme by not having a separate custodian. This doesn't guarantee a scheme can't happen, but it's an extra precaution and buffer than can make it much more difficult to happen. It also provides an important safety check. If your advisor sends you performance information about your account, you can go online any minute and double-check their figures.

- **Who pays your fees?** If your financial advisor is giving you "free" advice because they're attached to, or working for your bank etc., you should know these advisors usually earn commissions from the investments they sell you. They may recommend investments based on their, or the banks' best interest, not yours. Over time, being in the wrong investments may actually cost you more than paying a fee-only advisor.

- **Do they hold to a fiduciary standard?** Are they registered with the SEC? If so this requires that they act in your best interest, that they "do the right thing." Investment or financial advisors who are registered with the SEC, or a state securities regulator, are fiduciaries, subject to the duty of loyalty and due care with their clients. Typically, they are compensated by asset management fees and are expected to "always act" in the best interests of their clients.

- **What kind of tax hit are you looking at if you invest with them?** Inquiring about taxes and fees is a way to explore what your estimated net return might be. Ultimately what you really want to know is how much of the money you make do you get to keep after fees and after taxes? You want an advisor who has your tax bill in mind when they're making financial decisions for you. Most advisors will make a point to know and advise you about the tax ramifications relating to their management of your accounts.

Financial Master Robert Kiyosaki tells his followers to "separate those who say from those who do." His top three pieces of advice for those looking for a financial advisor are:

Look for someone who practices what they preach. Practicing what you preach is about distinguishing between those people who are openly giving their advice, such as a financial "expert," a speaker or instructor, or a media commentator and someone who is walking the talk and doing what they preach. Kiyosaki says, "Many of the so-called financial experts you'll encounter are making a living from selling or offering their advice, not practicing it.

The question I would ask before acting on their advice is: Are they taking their own advice? Are they investing in what they recommend you invest in? Are they practicing the habits and strategies they are advocating? Are they living their message daily? When it comes to brokers, does your real estate broker invest in real estate? Did your stockbroker purchase the same shares of stock he or she is recommending you buy?"

Find out whether this person is an actual financial advisor, or a glorified salesperson. Always follow the money. There is a big difference between a true financial adviser and a salesperson. Does the person advising you have no agenda, meaning they do not financially benefit, directly or indirectly from your investment choices? Or do they have an agenda of their own (meaning they will make a commission or fee from what they are selling you)?

There's nothing wrong with being a good salesperson. I work with many excellent salespeople. They make me money, and I make them money. However, the red flags go up when I meet someone claiming to be a "financial adviser" but, in reality, they are only recommending what they are paid a commission on. To figure out what they're really doing, just ask the question, "How do you get paid?"

Transaction versus Relationship. When it comes to stock brokers, real estate brokers and business brokers, you can generally separate the good from the not-so-good by how they approach your potential purchase.

Kiyosaki makes it easy to determine whether you're a transaction for someone (a one-time sale), or if they are in it for a long-term relationship where they care about you, your investment and your business. For instance, if you're talking with a broker or agent whom you've never met before, pay attention to the conversation. Are they only talking about this one deal, or this one buy? If so, he says, then chances are they are only in it for the short-term commission from that one transaction. You may never hear from this person again. To them you're just a dollar-sign and a commission. There's no way they have your best interests at heart.

If, on the other hand, this agent or broker is asking a lot of questions, and seems interested in your long-term plans and goals, they may be after a relationship. If they're talking about other future potential purchases and encouraging you to talk instead of them dominating the conversation, then they're probably more interested in developing a long-term business relationship with you and are more likely to have your best interests in mind. That's who you want to work with, and most often, that's who will give you good advice that's good for you, not just them.[30]

You can find an independent fee advisor by going to: findyourindependentadvisor.com and then simply entering your zip code.

BUDGET BASICS

Call it a budget, or a spending plan, or whatever works so you'll actually look at your money and plan what to do with it, but here are the basic steps to creating a plan that will bring your money into your direct control:

EVALUATE YOUR INCOME

How much money do you have coming in? Your paycheck is a given, but there are other sources: a second job, alimony, child support, yard sales, or sale of a car, baby-sitting, allowance from parents, trust fund if you're lucky or any other miscellaneous cash that you might have coming in. Write it all down and add it up. You don't need anything fancy. A yellow legal pad, a notebook, even a loose sheet of paper will work. You can go all out and create a spreadsheet if that works. But don't get

---

[30] https://www.richdad.com/three-principles?feed=RichDadNews

distracted by what you're going to create this list on. Just write it down. Easy.

CALCULATE YOUR EXPENSES

Writing down your income was easy, right? Now comes the part where most people stand up from the table and walk away, sweating, shaking, and sometimes even crying. Calculating your expenses is one of the most difficult steps in establishing a budget. This step forces you to look at how much money you're spending and what you're spending it on. Ouch. To move forward and get control of your money you need to know how much money is coming in, but more importantly how much is going out.

Begin by making a list of all your fixed expenses. This should include:

- You-Make yourself a bill (Pay Yourself First)
- Rent
- Mortgage payments
- Car payments
- Childcare expenses
- Insurance
- Utilities
- Cable
- Other subscription services

Next, include *variable expenses* such as food, gas, that $6 Starbucks latte you buy every morning, entertainment, etc. Make sure you don't forget miscellaneous and maintenance expenses such as property taxes, car maintenance, tag renewals, birthday gifts, etc. Once you've added up your outgoing monthly expenses, subtract them from your income and that'll tell you whether you're spending more than you earn. You'll also get a better idea of where you can cut back. Hard, but you can get through it. Take it in steps if you have to, listing the fixed expenses first.

If, like many of us you spend a few dollars here, a few dollars there, just keep track of all your receipts for a week. They'll give you a good idea of what you're buying on a regular basis.

TRIM THE FAT

Lucky you. The hardest part is done. You've listed your expenses and have taken a good hard look at where your money is going. Now it's time to look at where you can cut back on your spending, assign your dollars 'jobs' they do every month, and figure out how to put away money into savings rather than wants.

I had a caffeine junkie client who was surprised to find she was spending almost $6 a day on diet sodas, anywhere from $1.50 to $1.89 per bottle or cup. Depending on her stress levels on any given day, she might have two, three and sometimes four times sodas a day. That was almost $160 a month! Her $6 Starbucks every morning was another $180 a month. Just by eliminating sodas and making coffee at home and switching to tea instead of soda, she reduced her drink expenses from $340 a month to $40. That $300 she saved went into savings. She didn't really need the sugar anyway, she said. Later, she switched to water and was just as happy. Once she saw the numbers, $340 a month or $4,080 a year start gathering and compounding interest, the decision was easy to stick with.

Not all decisions are so obvious or easy, but one way to see where you may be able to cut costs is to evaluate which expenses are actually "needs" versus things you want or that would be "nice-to-haves." Sometimes those daily lattes taste better when they become a treat, or a once-a-week expense instead of a daily expense. If you're a pizza and a movie fan several nights a week, maybe you make your own pizza instead of ordering it delivered. You can subscribe to Amazon Prime or Hulu more reasonably than renting individual movies. Of course, if you only watch a movie or two a month, it might be less expensive to just rent the movie.

Having a budget and watching where your money goes will help you figure out the best way you can save money.

By looking at your daily and weekly expenditures in terms of 'needs' or 'wants' you can cut the expenses that aren't necessarily "needs." Other ways to scale back on your overall spending and/or design a better budget include finding those small drains on your money you don't really notice:

- Start monitoring your spending with a budgeting app that gives you a friendly reminder or alert if you're spending more than you should be in any one category.

- Shop around to see if you could secure a cheaper contract with your existing service providers. Can you negotiate or find a less expensive cell phone or internet plan? Do you qualify for lower rates or discounts on the services you have now?

- Are you paying for apps or websites that you don't use? Maybe you have a Netflix account, but watch most of your movies on Amazon Prime. Do you really need to subscribe to Star, Hulu, or other services when you only watch a couple movies a month there? Is it cheaper to just rent the movie you want to see — $2.99 versus paying $15 a month for a service you rarely use?

- Can you pay on your credit card bills more than once a month, or pay more than the minimum? Can you pay them off entirely? Speaking of credit cards—Dave Ramsey suggests eliminating credit cards entirely, but that may be extreme for your situation. If you have 20 cards or more, you might want to reduce that to two or three after making sure that doing so won't drop your credit score. If you can't give up your credit cards consider a balance-transfer credit card that offers a 0% introductory annual percentage rate to minimize the costs associated with any high-interest credit card debt you're carrying. (Note: Most balance transfers will cost a fee, usually around 2% to 5%.)

PAY YOURSELF FIRST

If you don't have a rainy-day fund, it's time to start one. In today's economic environment, you need money for emergencies. Ideally, you should have at least three to six months' salary in your emergency fund, but even having $1,000 as a backup is better than no backup at all. Emergencies are car or house repairs, medical expenses, and things that impact your ability to maintain a job, such as your health, your home, and transportation. While Dave Ramsey recommends a $1,000 a month emergency fund, I suggest a minimum of $5,000—especially if you own your home. A heater or furnace going out, or a leaky roof can wipe out your emergency savings fast. Aim for $1,000, then keep building.

By regularly saving and creating an emergency fund, it can make all the difference in the world when you're blindsided with an unexpected job loss or financial emergency. If you're struggling and only have a little to contribute to your savings each week, setting aside even $10 a week is better than nothing. Don't touch the money unless it's your last option. Sell things, get a second job, or do whatever you can before hitting that fund. It's easy to spend it, harder to save it.

PRACTICE DISCIPLINE AND STICK TO YOUR BUDGET

Creating a budget is a lot like joining a gym. It's easy in the beginning, but harder after the feelings of inspiration and motivation wears off. You can have a great budget and the perfect spending plan in place—but how do you stick to it? Discipline and dedication. You're going to make mistakes, and blow it, or spend it on the wrong things. If you have a significant other/spouse, you need to work together to hold each other accountable for any spending oversights. Give that accountability some teeth.

For instance, if one of you overspends, have a rule that the over spender contributes extra to next month's funds. Working together will make it easier to build the discipline you both need. If you're single, reach out to friends, create a savings support or accountability group.

If you take Dave Ramsey's Financial Peace courses you can meet other people there, online or in person, who are dedicated to the same savings and money management goals. It's not all hard work and no play. Create a reward for yourself for when you reach your goal. It might be a dinner out at a nice restaurant, or a short trip somewhere. Don't spend so much on the treat that you impact your savings but do reward yourself with something you want.

IMPROVE YOUR MONTHLY BUDGET'S CASH FLOW

If you are like most Americans, you receive a tax refund check every year. According to the IRS the average tax return refund in 2019 was about $3,000.00. I've seen some clients actually receiving $6,000.00, $8,000 and once over $10,000 back. You cannot afford to give Uncle Sam an interest-free loan every year. This refund represents tax money you overpaid to the government. If you fall into the average refund category, at a very minimum you could take that $250.00 per month that you pay to the IRS and incorporate that back into your paycheck. From there you can use that money to start your emergency fund, pay down credit card debt or increase your retirement IRA, Roth IRA or 401k. Talk to your accountant, CPA, employer or advisor about changing your withholding election and increase your take home pay immediately.

MONITOR YOUR CREDIT

One of the best side-effects of saving and spending wisely is that you will actually start enjoying keeping track of your credit score. A good credit score can be instrumental when it comes to controlling your finances. In case you really need financing for an emergency like buying a car if yours dies, you can qualify for the lowest interest rates. You can pull your credit report for free each year at AnnualCreditReport.com and view two of your credit scores at Credit.com.

If your credit is miserable or marginal you can try polishing it by disputing credit report errors and/or establishing a good payment history with a new line of starter credit, like a secured credit card or credit-builder loan. You can also work to pay down existing high debts.

Many consumers use a credit monitoring service. A credit monitoring service keeps track of changes in borrower behavior in order to notify consumers of potential fraud, as well as changes to their creditworthiness. Some services are free if you use a company's other services, and others are inexpensive, sometimes $5 to $15 a month. It's up to you to decide if such a service is for you.

COMPOUNDING

One of the best aspects of doing all the things I've listed above means you'll have money to save, which means if you put it in the right account, you'll have your money making money for you through the magic of compounding, or "compound interest," as it's often referred to.

Compound interest is interest that is earned on money that was previously earned as interest. So, if you have $100 and earn 5% on that money over a year, then you now have $105 in your account and have to do nothing other than leave the money in an account.

The next year you'll make 5% interest on $105, and each succeeding year after that you'll make interest on what is in your account. Even if you never touch this money again, it will continue to grow. This cycle perpetuates increasing interest and account balances at an increasing rate, sometimes known as exponential growth.

Compounding interest means you'll start earning interest on your initial deposit, and you'll earn interest on the interest you just earned.

You'll earn 5% on your original deposit $100 again. You'll earn 5% on the new $5 of interest earnings the bank paid to your account. That means you'll earn more than $5 next year because your account balance is now $105, even though you didn't make any deposits, so your earnings will accelerate.

With many banks, particularly online banks, you'll find that interest compounds daily and gets added to your account monthly, so the process moves even faster. If you add money monthly the process moves even faster. It takes a while to build momentum, but once you see your money increase it's very motivating to watch it build even more.

When it comes to compounding interest, time is your friend. You want to start as early as you can and leave your money in the account as long as you can. If you have a child, starting an account for them as soon as they're born can give them a tremendous head start. No matter what your age, it's never too late to start saving, but of course the longer you can save, the better off you'll be. Even five years on $200 a month can be a huge head start.

Of course, if you borrow money, the same principle (compounding) can work against you. Since you pay interest on money you borrowed, your loan balance can increase over time, even if you don't borrow any more money. This is why it's important to pay off credit card debt in full each month, and to consolidate debt and lower your interest rates when you can.

What Makes Compound Interest Powerful?

Compounding happens when interest is paid repeatedly. The first month, or year or two of compounding cycles aren't going to wow you. Unless you've deposited $50,000 or more, you'll wonder what all the hype is about. I promise you; the numbers pick up after you add interest over and over again.

How Often: There are different frequencies of compounding, including daily, weekly, monthly etc. How frequently your money is compounded, the more dramatic the results. To start with, open a savings account that compounds daily. You might only see interest payments on a monthly basis, but you can calculate them daily. Some accounts only calculate interest monthly or annually.

How Long: Time, and lots of it, is what makes compounding so magical and so much more dramatic. The longer the compounding period, the higher the numbers you'll see. Leave that money alone to make more money.

Interest Rates: Not all compounding is equal. You need to factor in the interest rate — the most important factor. Is the interest rate a 'nominal rate' or a 'real' rate? Higher rates obviously mean more money so it's important to understand the difference between the two.

A 'real interest rate' factors the inflation rate into account. Linking nominal and real interest rates can be approximated in the following equation: nominal rate = real interest rate + inflation rate, or nominal rate - inflation rate = real rate. "Nominal interest rate" refers to the interest rate before taking inflation into account. "Nominal" may also refer to the advertised or stated interest rate on a loan, without taking into account any fees or compounding of interest.

To avoid losing money through inflation, investors consider the real interest rate, rather than the nominal rate. For example, if the nominal interest rate offered on a three-year deposit is 4% and the inflation rate over this period is 3%, the investor's real rate of return is 1%. Conversely, if the nominal interest rate is 2% in an environment of 3% annual inflation, the investor's purchasing power erodes by 1% per year.[31]

However, an account with compounding and a lower nominal rate can end up with a higher balance than an account using a simple calculation.

---

[31] https://www.investopedia.com/terms/n/nominalinterestrate.asp

Just take a few minutes to do the math so you can figure out if that will happen, and then locate the breakeven point.

Withdrawals and Deposits: Withdrawals and deposits can also affect your account balance negatively or positively, but they are separate from compounding. Letting your money grow or continually adding new deposits to your account works best. If you choose to withdraw your earnings, you dampen the effect of compounding.

The amount of money you have to save does not affect compounding. If you begin with $100 or $1 million, compounding works the same way. You are earning a percentage of what you invest. Larger amounts earn the same percentage, but 5% of $500 looks a lot less than 5% of $5,000. That's why your earnings will seem bigger when you start with a large deposit. You aren't penalized for starting small or keeping accounts separate. Focus on percentages and time, as in, 'how much will you earn, and for how long?'

APY

APY stands for Annual Percentage Yield (APY), or the real rate of return earned on a savings deposit or investment. This factors in the effect of compounding interest. Unlike simple interest, compounding interest is calculated periodically, and the amount is immediately added to the balance. Daily or monthly compounding helps, especially if you're a new investor or new to compounding, but don't get confused by the numbers. Whether interest compounds daily or weekly or monthly, you still earn more or less the same APY. For example, an account paying 5% APY doesn't pay 5% per day. You get 1/365th of 5% every day. Still, frequent compounding gives you a little edge to help your money grow faster.

CHAPTER FIVE
COMPOUNDING AND THE "PIZZA AND A SIX-PACK" INVESTMENT STRATEGY TO AMASSING MONEY

"Any patient investor can turn five thousand dollars a year into nearly one million dollars. It's all about compounding."
~ Ronald S. Baron

When I first entered the Financial Services industry in 1984, I was hired by First Investors Corporation as a manager trainee. At the age of 25 I thought I was somewhat financially savvy. After all, I had lived on my own since the age of 20 and had my own stock account at age 18. I knew a lot of close friends who owned a good bit of real estate and I always tried to surround myself with individuals that I could learn from.

Accepting a position with First Investors was the start of my financial career. But there were still a lot of things I had to learn—the most important and fascinating lesson being around The Rule of 72, or "compounding." In a nutshell, the more frequently your money earns interest, the faster and bigger your balance will grow. As the interest earned is added to your account, you earn interest on the original balance, plus the previously earned interest. It truly is a case of your money working for you.

When interest is compounded, the amount paid in a year is actually more than the simple interest rate that is given. Financial institutions show the return as the APY (the final return on your money)—the actual annual return on an investment when compound interest is considered.

The Rule of 72 is an easy, straightforward way to determine how long an investment will take to double, given a fixed annual rate of interest. Investors can quickly get an estimate by simply dividing 72 by the annual rate of return. For example, $10,000.00 @ 3% would double in 24 years (72 divided by 3% = 24) or $10,000.00 @ 10% would double in 7.2 years (72 divided by 10 =7.2).

I was taught about compounding in such a way that if an individual starts with small increments of money, on a monthly basis they would be potential millionaires at retirement. So how much were we recommending everyone to put away regularly? Would you believe $25.00 dollars a week, or in those days we equated this cost to the individual as a "Pizza and a Six Pack," or about $100 per month. Pizza and beer prices in many parts of the country haven't changed much. You can still get a pizza for $14 to $25 and a six pack of beer for $6-$10.00 Let's stick with the $25 a week, $100 a month for the sake of ease in watching your investment. If you want to use $50 a week or $200 a month, you can do that too.

If you're not a beer and pizza person, use lattes and scones, wine or martinis, whatever you do indulge in regularly. The point is to find a number you feel comfortable investing weekly.

The rate of return we used then was 12% due to the economy and what CDs and other investments were earning at the time. Various older financial books may still show compounding using this return. However, I feel more comfortable using a return of 10% instead. So, let's start with investing basics:

- Interest
- Compounding (Rule of 72)
- Investing 101 (Basics)

WHAT IS INTEREST?

Interest is just rent people pay on money. Let's say I want to borrow $100 for a year. There's nothing in it for you to just loan me the money, but what if I agree to pay you an extra $5 (rent) at the end of that year? You agree, and you loan me the $100 (which is called the principal) with 5% due at the end of the year (that 5% on top of the principal is called the interest.), We're using a 5% return over time for this equation. David Bach relates to saving money monthly by equating your savings to the cost of a daily latte and a scone, or the first hour of your pay daily. It's where he got the name for his book, *The Latte Factor.*

Let's say you have saved $1,000 (your principal) from a part time job or by selling items at a garage sale. It doesn't matter how you earn it. You have $1,000. You put it into an interest earning account. It earns 5% (interest rate or earnings) once a year or (the compounding frequency for that account). At the end of the first year, you would have $1,050: your original principal, plus 5%, or $50. The second year, you would have $1,102.50. That's based upon the fact that your next interest payment equals 5% of $1,050, or $52.50. Pretty cool right? You've done nothing but let your money sit in the account. Your money is making you money!

Now, what do you do with that money once you've set it aside? You put it where it will continue to compound.

COMPOUNDING:

Compounding is the process in which an asset's earnings, your savings, your capital gains or interest, are reinvested to generate additional earnings over time.

For example, what if you could save $25.00 per week x 4 = $100.00 a month, or $25.00 per week x 52, for a total of $1300.00 per year. Finding a little fat in your budget isn't difficult if you know where to look.

Maybe you smoke. Factor in the cost of a pack or two of cigarettes a day—$8.91 in Connecticut or $10.45 a pack in New York. It doesn't matter what you use to wrap your head around the amount of savings you could see, just find something you can relate to, multiply by 5 (days of the work week) or (4 times per month)or (weekly x 52)and then that total times a 10 percent compounding return. If you simply invested $25.00 per week x 52 weeks at 10 percent and started at age 21 year you would have accumulated $848,433.00 at the age of 65. With $30.00 per week times 10 percent interest, that extra $5.00 per week, would accumulate to $1,018,120.00 at 65. As the accumulated interest goes up, compounding keeps kicking in. Even the amount you've saved in five years will astound you.

Imagine how much you could see those numbers go up if you added an extra $250, $500 or $1,000 a year, or a month for 20, 30, or 40 years. That's why compounding is so wonderful. On the negative side, if you have $1,000 in credit card debt, that same compounding is happening to and against you. Especially if your credit card interest is between 14-28 percent. You can end up paying more than the item originally cost. It's a good reason why you should pay off your credit cards in full every month, so the interest doesn't compound and hurt you.

Compounding is great. Now, how do you start compounding your long-term savings? Start with your employer's 401K program, especially if they match your savings, and even if they don't. If you set it up right it's taken right off the top, before federal tax and before you even see it appear in your paycheck. It's automatic.

If you're self-employed or a small business owner, consider a Simplified Employee Pension (SEP), Individual 401k, Simple IRA, a Roth or Individual IRA. More information about all those things is listed at the end of this book. If you feel uncertain or intimidated by the process or picking the best place to put your savings, consider hiring a financial advisor to get you started.

INVESTING

According to Sapling.com, "Investing is a way to increase the amount of money you have by putting it into financial products. These products include bank accounts, money market accounts, stocks, bonds, mutual funds, ETF's, precious metals and property. Anything with the potential to increase in value can be an investment.

That's it. Simple, right? Well, on the surface it is. Picking the right investment is where the art of investing comes in. Warren Buffett bought his first stock at age 11 using the information available to any other investor at the time. Now well into his eighties, he's still investing. And, while he's the king of investing, he's not a magician, nor does he have any unique talents. He doesn't hide his investments either. Seven of the 10 are banks or financials. The remaining three (Apple, Coca-Cola, and Kraft Heinz) are large consumer brands. Here are his largest holdings:

- Apple (NASDAQ: AAPL)
- Bank of America (NYSE: BAC)
- Wells Fargo (NYSE: WFC)
- Coca-Cola (NYSE: KO)
- American Express (NYSE: AXP)
- Kraft Heinz (NASDAQ: KHC)
- U.S. Bancorp (NYSE: USB)
- JPMorgan Chase (NYSE: JPM)
- Moody's (NYSE: MCO)
- Bank of New York Mellon (NYSE: BK)[32]

He does have a 7-step process he follows that you'd do well to follow also:

- Invest in what you know.

---

[32] https://www.fool.com/investing/warren-buffett-stocks-investing-advice.aspx

- Learn the basics of value investing.
- Identify cheap stocks.
- Find businesses that will stand the test of time.
- Invest in good management.
- Be aggressive during tough times.
- Keep a long-term mind-set.[33]

Let's look at those steps in more detail:

Invest in what you know. Have you noticed a theme yet? It's "education." Learn all you can about your money, your interest, and about investing. Be familiar with the terms, the names, the buzz words, and everything there is to know about investing. It's a life-long process, but you can pick up the basics in a course, online, through books, or extensive reading. If you want to get to know Warren Buffet and how he thinks about investing, here are five of the best books I'd recommend about him. He has a net worth of 80 billion dollars, so it's a good idea to learn about how he thinks:

- *Buffett: The Making of an American Capitalist, by Roger Lowenstein*
- *The Warren Buffett Way, by Robert G. Hagstrom*
- *The Warren Buffett CEO, by Robert P. Miles*
- *The Snowball: Warren Buffett and the Business of Life, by Alice Schroeder*
- *Tap Dancing to Work: Warren Buffett on Practically Everything, 1966-2013, by Carol J. Loomis*

Learn the Basics of Value Investing.

The investment strategy categorized as "value investing" involves picking stocks that appear to be trading for less than their intrinsic or book

---

[33] https://www.fool.com/investing/how-to-invest-warren-buffett-step-by-step-guide.aspx

value. As Investopedia explains, "Value investors actively ferret out stocks they think the stock market is underestimating. They believe the market overreacts to good and bad news, resulting in stock price movements that do not correspond to a company's long-term fundamentals. The overreaction offers an opportunity to profit by buying stocks at discounted prices—on sale."[34]

If you're a bargain shopper for instance, value investing should make sense. Let's say you find a certain brand of large screen television at a brand name store. It's selling for $1,200. But you keep looking around and lo and behold, you find the same brand, same size, same television on sale at Wal-Mart or Costco. It's the same television, but at half or two thirds the price. Value stocks are the same sort of thing. In the stock market, the equivalent of a stock being cheap or discounted is when its shares are undervalued. Value investors hope to profit from shares they perceive to be deeply discounted.[35]

Buffett is considered one of, if not the best value investor in the world. He's using the same information and tools that you can. He just uses them very well.

Identify cheap stocks.

Once you've established your value-investing criteria, make a wish list of stocks you'd like to invest in. You'll need to understand some basic terms like **PB**- Price to Book, **PE**-Price to Earnings Ratio, **PEG**-Price / Earnings-to- Growth ratio, **EPS**, - Earning Per Share, Dividend Payout Ratio, Momentum and the significance of Quarterly Earnings Reports. All these terms and many more can be found on Investopedia.com. Sign up for their free "Term of the day".

---

[34] https://www.investopedia.com/terms/v/valueinvesting.asp
[35] https://www.investopedia.com/terms/v/valueinvesting.asp

Just remember one basic principle. In most cases when a company misses their quarterly earnings by a penny or even if they just meet the earnings that were projected, the stock usually will fall upon the announcement. This fall may not signal a, "Time to Buy". Under normal situations, only after a company starts to post positive or consecutive positive earnings above their projection will the company's stock price rise.

Be careful not to, "Catch a Falling Knife". Put simply, this represents a company whose price will keep falling while bad news is prevalent, and earnings are not meeting the company's own estimates.

Find Businesses That Will Stand the Test of Time. Once you have a list of stocks whose metrics look attractive, narrow it down by choosing businesses that will hold up well during recessions. You won't catch them all, and probably not the most unlikely — as Airstream Trailers' success during the great recession. But you'll do better when it comes to investing. This is why Buffett loves to invest in utilities. If the company's success depends on a strong economy, or luxury demand, you may not do as well, so eliminate these companies from your list.

Invest in Good Management. Warren Buffett will invest in a stock only if he trusts management and thinks it will continuously act in shareholders' best interest. Pay attention to the CEO, and a company's history. Look for positive indicators, like a history of dividend growth and buybacks (both ways of returning capital to investors), and excellent reputations. Buffett has bought and sold investments based solely on management actions. If the people running a company are good managers, then the rest will follow.

Be Aggressive During Tough Times. Life is a series of thunderstorms and rainbows. No matter what the economy is doing, there's going to come a time when dark clouds darken in the market. Buffett invests money in good times and bad and does well and poorly in good times and bad. That's how it goes. He did a great job of capitalizing on opportunities during and shortly after the Great Recession, with such savvy deals as his Bank of America investment. He's practical and nonplussed about the market. He said in one annual letter to his shareholders, "Every decade or so, dark clouds will fill the economic skies, and they will briefly rain gold." Long-term investors buying the right companies will likely do just fine over the long haul.

It's important, Buffett says, to look for opportunities during tough economic times.[36] I often tell my clients that one of the secrets of successful long-term investors is that, like Buffett and most of the other Financial Masters I've listed, they love market corrections, as they offer the best opportunities for the savvy investor.

Keep a Long-Term Mindset

There are a lot of ways to make money in the stock market, but the best way is to make it over time. In regard to Berkshire Hathaway's stock portfolio, Buffett has said that "our favorite holding period is forever." Buffett and his team sell stocks regularly, and there are a variety of good reasons for selling your holdings, but until you understand investing, stocks and the process, it's best to go into investing with a long-term mentality. In other words, if you can't see yourself owning the stock for years, don't buy it at all. "If you aren't willing to own a stock for 10 years, don't even think about owning it for 10 minutes," Buffett has said. Buying stocks because you think they're going to have a good quarter, or because a hot new product is being released next year, is not how Warren Buffet has made his millions.

Obviously, I cannot explain everything there is to know about stocks or investing in this book, let alone in one chapter. There are thousands of magazines, books, courses, and other resources that will do a far better

---

[36] https://www.fool.com/investing/how-to-invest-warren-buffett-step-by-step-guide.aspx

job of that. I'm just trying to give you a basic overview, so you have an advantageous starting point.

Now, while Warren Buffet has made his money with his process, that doesn't mean it's the only successful model out there. Billionaire Ron Baron says he tripled his normal stock investments during the fall 2019 market volatility. He doesn't invest like Buffett, or like most financial investors.

In fact, he says, "financial advisers are always buying at the wrong time and selling at the wrong time." "It's because they're emotional." "In the first week of August, when the market was acting erratic and it had fallen sharply, I tripled the investment that I make every month in the funds that week," Baron Capital said in a "Squawk Box" interview.[37] He may be less risk averse than Buffett, but he does make his fortune on value investing just as Buffett does. Like Buffett, Baron has made a fortune by doing extensive research, buying the stocks of companies he feels are undervalued, and keeping them for an average of about 14 years.[38] The proof of his risk process and value investing is in his holdings. He started Baron Capital in 1982. The investment firm currently has around $30 billion in assets under management.

---

[37] https://www.cnbc.com/2019/08/20/ron-baron-says-he-tripled-normal-stock-buys-during-recent-wild-swings.html
[38] https://www.cnbc.com/2019/08/20/ron-baron-says-he-tripled-normal-stock-buys-during-recent-wild-swings.html

CHAPTER SIX
ASSETS AND LIABILITIES AND WHY YOU SHOULD NEVER OWN ANYTHING YOU CAN RENT

Don M., a well-known orthopedic surgeon who made over a million dollars a year only a few years out of Medical School, has one financial tip that works for everyone. "I never buy what I can rent, or hire, and I only buy things that appreciate in value," he said. It's not the purchase of items that costs you, he explained. It's the maintenance of them. "If you have to buy something, buy the best. It requires less maintenance, retains its value, and you can resell it for almost what you paid for it."

The son of a dirt-poor farmer in North Carolina, Don had struggled most of his life, borrowing or bartering for whatever he needed growing up. That, he said, was the secret to his being able to afford college and later, medical school. He maintained the practice of not buying what he could rent and hiring people to do what allowed him to maximize his time. The money he saved by not owning, maintaining, and repairing tools, cars, equipment, and sports gear was invested in the stock market and real estate.

He held to this financial strategy throughout his marriage and after he retired. While his friends collected expensive lawn tools, and did their own yard work and repairs, Don focused on maximizing his time in his practice, and on learning about investing. It paid off handsomely. Don understood the concept of assets and liabilities off of paper as well as on paper.

Don echoed what Bob Gardiner, or Robert "Stretch" Gardiner, the former head of Dean Witter [which later became Morgan Stanley] said about what you do decide to buy.

David Bach was working at Morgan Stanley when Gardiner came and spoke to their clients. Bach wanted to spend more time with him and offered to take him to the airport. On the way to the airport of course he asked him for advice! Who wouldn't? Always seize the opportunity to learn from the masters! Anyway, Bach said he asked Gardiner for his best advice and he said, "the secret to building wealth is to buy quality and don't buy crap. And if you buy quality and leave it alone, it will make you wealthy."

That's not exactly an insider's stock tip, but it's worth even more. It's basic life advice that if followed, can make you wealthy.

Assets

What are assets? In financial accounting, all resources owned by the business fit the definition of an asset. Any tangible or intangible thing that can be owned or controlled to produce value by a company is considered an asset. To distill it down, assets represent value of ownership that can be converted into cash. If you aren't a business, but are an individual the same is true. Any item or items of value that belong to an individual are classified as personal assets. These can also be any other thing with a cash value. When someone goes to a bank or other institution to apply for loans, their personal assets and the values given to those are often considered. These assets can be motor vehicles, tools, artwork, art collections, electronics, antiques, real estate or other valuable items.

Personal assets are the foundation of the formula for net worth for consumers. When talking about personal finance, an individual's wealth can be measured in terms of the total value of the property and cash they own. Understanding your net worth and knowing what assets you have and their valuation is an important part of understanding your financial situation, and planning for your future.

The value of your personal assets can be higher or lower than you expect. It depends on whether your assets are:

Tangible Property

This a term in law that is defined as property that is physical (can be touched), is not real property, and can be physically relocated. These assets include your vehicles, cell phones, computers, furniture, tools, office equipment and other furnishings. They also include your miscellaneous assets such as jewelry, toys, collectibles, and sports equipment. Many of these assets decline in value over time, but some, such as your collectibles, may appreciate over time.

Tangible assets also include your financial assets such as stocks and bonds that have a transactional exchange value. The value of these assets and their liquidity may vary regularly depending on the market for their exchange.

The tax law reflects that most tangible business property depreciates over time. The law provides a series of class lives for these assets, but most are depreciated over three, five and seven-year periods. (Special rules allow accelerated write-offs)

Real Property

These assets would include a home, a rental property, land and other physical property. The value of these assets will vary based upon location, maintenance, and other market conditions. They may appreciate or depreciate. These assets generally have a much longer life than tangible assets. In fact, the tax code generally provides class lives of 27.5 to 39 years for buildings depending on whether their use is residential or non-residential.

Intangible Property

Personal intangible assets include any of your assets that derive their value from contractual claims, such as patents. While tangible assets generally have a specific transactional value, intangible assets have a theoretical value. These assets are most often associated with a business. They include assets such as brand name value, intellectual property (trademarks/ patents/copyrights/know-how), goodwill and other assets that don't have a "physical" nature. However, they can prove very valuable for a business and can be critical to its long-term success or failure.

For example, Coca-Cola, Pepsi, or other major soda brands wouldn't be nearly as successful if it not for the money made through the recognition of their name and brand. Although brand recognition isn't a physical asset that can be seen or touched, it can have a meaningful impact on generating sales.[39]

Spreading your wealth around in a variety of assets (diversifying) is smart. That way if something suffers or decreases in value, some of the other assets may offset this by outperforming or increasing in value. Once you identify and list your assets it's a good idea to name and number them and include as many details as possible about them as possible. You can do this by hand, or digitally. Information about

---

[39] https://www.investopedia.com/terms/i/intangibleasset.asp

deeds, bills of sale, titles, insurance policies, and so forth should be included. To ensure your property's safety, you should keep or scan as many receipts as possible, especially on high-ticket items. Any information that proves ownership should also be maintained. The names and contact information of the people (family members, attorneys, CPA, etc.) who are authorized to handle these assets should also be included.[40]

Assets that have a value that cannot be easily accessed (art, antiques, vehicles, etc.) are also included in the personal asset's category. Financial experts warn against placing all or the majority of your personal assets into a single asset type or location.

Additionally, such assets can become liabilities if they are not well taken care of or managed. Sometimes owners of personal assets may use them to create income.

Liabilities

What are liabilities? According to Investopedia and most experts, liabilities are defined as an individual's or company's legal financial debts or obligations that arise during business operations. Here are some examples of liabilities: loans, accounts payable, mortgages, deferred revenues, earned premiums, unearned premiums, and accrued expenses. These liabilities are different than "being liable," as in a court case or other legal action. When creating your budget or spending plan it's important to know what your liabilities are, and how you plan to deal with them. The fewer liabilities you have, the better.

---

[40] https://www.upcounsel.com/personal-assets

One of the controversial investing strategies around assets and liabilities is the belief that you should never own a home that you yourself live in. That runs counter to what most of us believe, since owning our own home is part of the American dream. And for many, it is.

This controversial belief around not owning your home revolves around the thought that you might want to own a house as an investment and rent it out to others to earn income. It's possible to own a business that owns an apartment building in which you live. However, owning a building that's primary purpose is to simply house you is something you should never do.

The SimpleDollar.com has a great article that details all the pros and cons of home ownership that I advise everyone to read. I've put the link at the end of the book in the resource section.

Once you've gotten your money under control and you're at the point of deciding where to invest the money you're saving, it's important to have clearly defined goals based on where you want to be in five years, ten, or at retirement. Financial master Tony Robbins advises people to think about 'asset allocation.' Asset allocation is the process you use to decide how to break up, or 'divvy up' your resources or assets. The trick, Robbins says, is allocating your assets in such a way that brings you the maximum reward with the minimum amount of risk. Doing this also assures diversification, which protects your portfolio from sudden changes in the market.

Enter Robbins' three buckets:

- Your Security Bucket
- Your Risk/Growth Bucket
- Your Dream Bucket

Your Security Bucket

Your Security Bucket is just what it sounds like—your Security, or Peace of Mind Bucket. This is your low to no risk, save up for the winter, protect your assets bucket. It's nothing exciting, won't turn heads or impress anyone, but it will protect your nest egg and insure you have the funds to retire well, and live protected financially. Essentially, Robbins says, your Security Bucket is where you want to keep the part of your nest egg you can't afford to lose. Therefore, you can consider it to be a sanctuary of safe investments you lock up tight, leave alone, and then hide the key.

You may wonder what type of investments would you find in, or allocate to your Security Bucket? Investment options with low volatility are ideal. Options include:

1. Cash/Cash Equivalents (such as money market funds with checking privileges)
2. Bonds (such as TIPS, Treasury inflation-protected securities)
3. Market-linked CDs
4. Your home – Definitely an asset, but not an investment. This is your sacred safe haven—something that you shouldn't be "spending"!
5. Your Pension (if you're fortunate enough to have one)
6. Guaranteed Annuities (a good one!)
7. Your life insurance policy
8. Structured Notes (One with 100% principal protection, purchased through a Registered Investment Advisor)

These investments grow slowly, especially at first, but the power of compounding means you can find investments with maximum rewards in a secure environment.[41]

Your Risk/Growth Bucket

Your Risk/Growth bucket is exactly what it sounds like, high risk, exciting, sexy with the potential for high, rich, amazing returns. If your Security Bucket is an old station wagon (old, slow, and dependable), your Risk Bucket is a sports car (beautiful and fast). You can win races with your Risk Bucket speedster, but you might also end up on the side of the road waiting for road service. Like a scratch lottery ticket, you can be rewarded for your risk in certain investments, or you can also lose everything. The bottom line is, anything you put in your Risk/Growth bucket comes with the caveat that you must be prepared to lose it, particularly if you don't have protective measures in place. There are seven main asset classes to consider, and here are some that fall into those categories:

1. **Equities** – Another word for stocks, or ownership shares of individual companies or vehicles for owning many of them at once, like mutual funds, indexes, and exchange-traded funds (ETFs).
2. **High-Yield Bonds** (aka junk bonds)
3. **Real Estate**
4. **Commodities** (gold, silver, oil, coffee, cotton, etc.)
5. **Currencies**
6. **Collectibles**

---

[41] https://www.tonyrobbins.com/wealth-lifestyle/asset-allocation/

7. **Structured Notes** (anything without 100% principal protection)

Depending on your success or failure, it can be easy to get caught up when you're winning, and ignore your losses. Pay attention to your risk bucket. It's a mix of wins and losses that determines your success.[42]

Your Dream Bucket

Yep, the purpose of the Dream Bucket is to have fun. While you're protecting, investing, and risking, you should also be setting aside something for yourself and your family, so you enjoy life as well. Your Dream Bucket's purpose is to excite you, to put some juice in your life so you want to earn and contribute even more. The items you're saving for in your Dream Bucket should be considered strategic splurges.

Be creative! What can you not stop dreaming about? What makes you want to cry when you visualize yourself achieving it? It could be season tickets to your favorite sports team or theatre. Or a new car, maybe one that isn't so practical. It could be handing over the deed to a new home to your parents and treasuring the look on their faces. If you're a frequent flyer, maybe you dream of upgrading from Economy to Business Class. Your imagination is the only limit.

Many people have a lot of money but not much lifestyle. While they may focus much of their lives to watching numbers accumulate in a bank account, they miss out on the joy along the way. Your dreams

---

[42] https://www.tonyrobbins.com/wealth-lifestyle/asset-allocation/

are not designed to give you a financial payoff; they are designed to give you a greater quality of life.

SO HOW DO YOU FILL YOUR DREAM BUCKET?

Robbins says there are three ways in which you can fill your dream bucket:

1. Jackpots – If you get a bonus or a windfall of some kind, you may want to fuel your dream tank with it.
2. Your Risk/Growth Bucket gets a positive hit and you score big. In this case, you may want to take some of the risk off the table and put one-third of the unexpected dividends into each bucket.
3. Save a percentage of your income and sock it away until you're able to purchase your dreams. This would be separate from what you're saving towards building your Money Machine. Implementing Tony Robbins' techniques will help you reach your goals faster.[43]

LORI GREINER ON INVESTING — LISTEN TO YOUR INTUITION

Women have a distinct advantage over men when it comes to investing and asset allocation. What is that? They're more likely to act on their intuition. I'm not saying that men aren't intuitive. Science tells us we're all intuitive, but because of cultural differences, that women are more encouraged to act on their intuition, or feelings. Men can be just as intuitive, as we've seen with Warren Buffet's

---

[43] https://www.tonyrobbins.com/wealth-lifestyle/asset-allocation/

success. If you're interested in intuition, I encourage you to read Financial master Lori Greiner's book, *Invent It, Sell It, Bank It* (Random House, 2014).

While there's a lot of science to successful investing, it's also highly subjective and intuitive. In her book and in numerous interviews, Greiner has said she can tell instantly if a product is a "hero or a zero." She's not just bragging. She's clearly shown through her many thriving investments and a 90% success rate on new items she's launched that she has a true knack for spotting winners. She's well known for her uncanny ability to know and identify emerging brands and invest in them. Several of her investments, including her most successful product, 'Scrub Daddy,' are among the highest success stories on *Shark Tank*.[44]

There's one more tip about investing that I found intriguing as I was doing research on investing. It comes from Napoleon Hill:

"Your personality is your greatest asset or liability. It embraces everything you control, your mind, your body, and your soul."
~ Napoleon Hill

Like Tony Robbins and most of the other financial masters, Hill advocates for investing in one's self as well as one's finances. His approach has more to do with improving your money mindset than your bottom line, but it can ultimately impact your bottom line, so I'm including it.

Your personality is your trademark or brand. Whether you work for a company or for yourself, your personality can serve as an asset or

---

[44] http://www.lorigreiner.com/meet-lori.html

a liability. With a positive mental attitude and use of the "The Big 3" traits of an attractive personality, you are sure to win in any given situation:

- Smile
- Facial expression
- Tone of voice

But those three traits come about as a result of what Hill calls "The 29 Factors of a Pleasing Personality."

- A Positive Mental Attitude
- Flexibility of the Mind
- Sincerity of Purpose
- Promptness of Decision
- Common Courtesy
- Tactfulness
- Pleasing Tone of Voice
- Facial Expression and the Habit of Smiling
- Tolerance
- Frankness in Manner of Speech
- A Keen Sense of Humor
- Faith in Infinite Intelligence
- A Keen Sense of Justice
- Appropriateness of Words
- Effective Speech
- Control of the Emotions
- Alertness of Interest
- Versatility
- Fondness for People

- Control of Temper
- Hope and Ambition
- Temperance
- Patience
- Humility of the Heart
- Appropriateness of Dress
- Effective Showmanship
- Clean Sportsmanship
- Ability to Shake Hands Properly
- Personal Magnetism

If you plan on accomplishing anything above a mediocre life, the financial masters all say in one way or another, you will need the cooperation and assistance of others along your journey. To get the help you need in reaching your goals you must become the kind of person others want to be around.[45]

Poet and Civil Rights Activist Maya Angelou famously quoted, "People will forget what you said, people will forget what you did, but people will never forget how you made them feel." Even though we may like to think all we need to become a financial success is skills with spreadsheets and numbers, the fact is, (according to Fuel-Design.com anyway), money is 20% how-to-skills and 80% emotional and intuitive and psychological.[46] So it's highly advisable to work on the whole package.

---

[45] http://www.naphill.org/focus-instructors/your-personality-asset-or-liability/
[46] https://www.fueldesign.co.nz/website-design-blog/buying_deci-sions_are_only_20-percent_logic_and_80-percent_emotional

CHAPTER SEVEN
WHEN TO PAY OFF DEBT, STUDENT
LOANS AND YOUR MORTGAGE

D ebt, like wealth, is a fascinating, magical, fearsome, and complex thing. Most of us have it, but not everyone understands it or how it works for or against us. That's why another one of the most frequently asked questions I get is, "Should I pay down my debt or save my money?" Financial master David Bach advises people both save and pay down their debt at the same time:

"In the real world, when I work with people who pay just their debt down and they don't save at the same time, what ultimately happens is after a year or two — because they don't see their net worth growing and they're only working on something negative — is it's depressing. They lose the motivation to keep doing it."

Bach told Business Insider that the plan is very simple. "Let's say you have an extra $100. Instead of putting the entire amount toward your credit card bill, dedicate $50 to paying off debt and put $50 in savings. Here's what happens: The debt starts to shrink, your savings start to grow," Bach explained. "You see yourself making progress—that will keep motivating you to keep going."[47]

---

[47] https://www.businessinsider.com/when-to-pay-back-credit-card-debt-2016-12

IS ALL DEBT BAD?

Listen to Suze Orman, Dave Ramsey and other money masters and they'll not only tell you that all debt is bad, but that it's downright evil. Robert Kiyosaki however will tell you debt is good. He'll tell you that he's millions of dollars in debt and yet "sleeps well at night."

Is debt the new money, or is it bad? Is there such a thing as "good debt"? Who's right? The fact is, debt can be good. I'm talking about certain kinds of debt, like the debt the rich work for, which is good debt, or investor debt. The poor pile up bad debt, or consumer debt, like credit card debt. Understanding what debt is, how it works, how it hurts and how it helps are critical to knowing what debt to pay off, what debt to take on, and how to manage your debt as well as you manage your income.

There are other reasons debt can be bad or good. Good debt can be an investment that may create value or generate long-term income. For instance, taking out student loans to pay for a college education is the perfect example of good debt. Because student loans typically have a very low interest rate compared to other types of debt you keep your debt lower. I'm sure some will argue differently, but a college education increases your value as an employee and raises your potential future income, even if you have to go into debt to finance it.

Bad debt is, well, "bad debt" because it's debt you've incurred to buy things that quickly lose their value and do not generate long-term income. Bad debt is also debt that likely carries a high interest rate, like credit card debt. The best rule of thumb to use in order to avoid bad debt is this: If you can't afford it and you don't need it, don't buy it. If you buy a fancy, $200 golf club, or a leather bomber jacket, or new shoes, etc. on your credit card, but you can't pay the balance on your card off for years, those shoes (with their compounded interest) will eventually cost you over $250. By the time that bad debt is paid off you may not even have the shoes, the club or the jacket.

WHEN TO PAY OFF YOUR MORTGAGE

Who doesn't want to own their home free and clear? It's why many couples will do whatever it takes to pay off their mortgage early. But should you? According to financial experts, there is actually a cost to your bottom line should you choose to pay off your mortgage early. Just do the math. The amount you'll save in interest by paying off your mortgage early probably won't exceed what you would earn in other long-term investments, such as stocks, mutual funds, and real estate. If you take a 30-year mortgage versus a 15-year mortgage your monthly payments will be lower, allowing you to invest your money in other opportunities or accounts.

In order for investments to be preferable to paying off a mortgage early, the annualized rate of return over a certain number of years would only need to make more than the mortgage interest. And since most people are sitting on relatively low mortgage rates, between 3.5 to 5.5%, beating that rate isn't tough. Unless you're a numbers whiz, or you enjoy playing with a calculator, interest rates and financial information, this is where a good financial advisor comes in handy. They can actually run the numbers and give you your options, then help you decide which approach and which mortgage is best for you.

Suze Orman, Kevin O'Leary of *Shark Tank*, David Bach and others will disagree with any approach that claims debt is "good." All those I listed are firm believers that "debt is evil" and that the sooner you're debt free, the better.

Dave Ramsey advocates a 15-year loan and paying off your mortgage as quickly as possible, but not at the cost of sacrificing your retirement savings. Ramsey tells his readers and listeners that they should first invest 15% of their income for retirement before they work toward paying off their mortgage.[48] His reasoning? If you focus on just paying off your

---

[48] Dave Ramsey. https://www.daveramsey.com/blog/pay-off-mortgage-or-save-retirement

mortgage over 15-30 years without paying into your retirement fund, you lose that 15-30 years of compounding interest and savings you'd have if you did both.

Some homeowners argue they could pay off the mortgage early and have more money to devote to retirement investing once they own their home free and clear. They forget, Ramsey says, the most important part of investing: the longer you invest, the more your money can grow.

Ramsey explains the situation in his blog, "Joe Homeowner decides to double up on his house payments instead of investing for retirement. He pays off his mortgage in 15 years, but he has zero retirement savings. To catch up with Jane, he'll have to invest $2,600 a month!"[49]

WHEN IS DEBT GOOD?

There is personal debt, and business debt. What might be bad debt for an individual could be very good debt for a business. For instance, the government encourages businesses to use debt by allowing businesses to deduct the interest on their debt from corporate income taxes. While the corporate tax rate is now 21%, it used to be at 35% (one of the highest in the world). This deduction is quite enticing—especially to a small business. It is quite possible for a company's cost of debt to drop below 5% after considering the tax break associated with interest.

Second, debt is a much cheaper form of financing than equity. Why? *The Harvard Business Review* explains it very succinctly:

- "Equity is riskier than debt. Because a company typically has no legal obligation to pay dividends to common shareholders, those shareholders want and expect a certain rate of return. Debt is much less risky for the investor because the firm is legally obligated to pay it.

---

[49] https://www.daveramsey.com/blog/pay-off-mortgage-or-save-retirement

- "Shareholders (those that provided the equity funding) are the first to lose their investments when a firm goes bankrupt. Finally, much of the return on equity is tied up in stock appreciation, which requires a company to grow revenue, profit and cash flow. An investor typically wants at least a 10% return due to these risks, while debt can usually be found at a lower rate."[50]

These facts make debt a bargain.

If you're still feeling confused about debt, and about when to pay off student loans or other debt, you're not alone. If you want to know the length of time to have a mortgage, or whether you should only buy a used car and never a new one, or if you should rent versus buying, or lease versus owning your vehicle, I likely can't help you without all of your financial facts. Every person's financial situation is different. I'd need the details of your plan, if you have one already, your income tax return info, debt summary, a spending plan outline and your goals to really be able to help you. However, what I can do is point you to the most common opinions by a variety of successful financial experts on the topic and encourage you to find your own answers or hire an advisor to help you.

The bottom line from all financial experts, self-included, is to avoid debt as much and as often as possible. Incur debt only when it's part of a conscious, strategic plan. Avoid bad debt like "payday loans" which charge up to 300% interest. Don't max out your credit cards. Sell, return, or resell items around your house to make money, or get a second or third job to avoid going into debt. Dave Ramsey's "debt snowball," is a good way to approach and eliminate debt, as are other strategies for reducing or eliminating debt. There's another option—The Debt Avalanche. Both methods require that you list out your debts and make minimum payments on all but one debt. In the debt avalanche method, you pay extra money toward the debt with the highest interest rate. When

---

[50] Harvard Business Review. https://hbr.org/2009/07/when-is-debt-good

dealing with the debt snowball, pay the smallest debt amount first and work your way up, regardless of interest rate.

Forbes, and other experts agree that if you're serious about paying off your debt the Debt Avalanche[51] is the best, fastest way to do it. The advantage of Dave Ramsey's Debt Snowball is that the focus is on building and maintaining the motivation to keep reducing your debt. Let's face it—paying off debt is not fun and it's hard to stay upbeat and excited about it—thus, the Debt Snowball. Even Ramsey agrees. He says, "The math seems to lean more toward paying the highest interest debts first. But what I have learned is that personal finance is 20% head knowledge and 80% behavior. You need some quick wins in order to stay pumped enough to get out of debt completely."[52]

You know yourself best. Do you have the discipline and motivation to pay off your debts without a built-in motivator? Then use the Avalanche approach. If you need nudging and support and immediate wins, then go with the Debt Snowball. There's no law saying you have to stick with one or the other if it's not working for you. If you discover you're plenty motivated without Ramsey's method, switch over, and vice versa.

One last thing. No one likes being in debt, especially if it's not part of your overall financial plan. That's why getting out of debt can be such a cause for celebration. Paying off that car loan, student loans, mortgage or other major debt can be a great reason to celebrate. So, go ahead and do that; just make sure that your celebration doesn't generate more debt. Buy a pizza, have a bonfire and burn something, have a party. Then get right back to figuring out how best to invest, save, and earn so you can retire on your terms.

---

[51] https://www.investopedia.com/articles/personal-finance/080716/debt-avalanche-vs-debt-snowball-which-best-you.asp

[52] https://www.investopedia.com/articles/personal-finance/080716/debt-avalanche-vs-debt-snowball-which-best-you.asp

CHAPTER EIGHT
MONEY REGRETS THROUGH
THE DECADES

"By failing to prepare, you are preparing to fail."
~ Benjamin Franklin

Regrets? We've all had a few, especially when it comes to money. Almost two thirds or (71%) of us have regrets about how we've managed our money, says a Harris poll posted by personal finance website NerdWallet. The poll says that millennials (those aged 18-34 in the survey) are more likely than other age groups to have financial regrets (83%). The poll also found millennials are more likely than generation X-ers and Baby Boomers to have such regrets (83%). [53]

What do people regret the most? Most say not planning early enough (48%), followed by spending too much on nonessentials (39%), credit-card debt (33%) and not having a budget (32%). This was a survey of only 2,000 U.S. adults, but still, the numbers are telling. The number one regret, not planning, impacts all age groups in so many areas, from retirement savings to the ability to save up for a down payment on a

---

[53] https://www.marketwatch.com/story/the-no-1-financial-regret-of-millennials-and-they-dont-have-many-2017-09-15

home. It's no surprise that baby boomers regret that the most (52%), followed by Gen Xer's (48%) and millennials (43%).

Do you have regrets? Do you worry about money? Whether your answer is yes, no, or sometimes, when you think about your past choices, you're not alone. According to a 2019 Gallup poll, only 25% of Americans say they "worry about money all the time" while the rest of us worry about money some of the time.

Those who worry "all the time," worry that "their household income won't be enough to cover their expenses."[54] 25% is a quarter of the population. Since more people are reporting they're saving more than ever before, that percentage tells me a lot of people are still struggling financially. Their pain is real.

Even for those who are better off and not thinking about money all the time, the number one cause of stress is still, you guessed it—money. According to a recent report from BlackRock, an investment management company, money worries rank higher than our worries about health, family and work. Baby Boomers may have more regrets about money, but BlackRock claims millennials worry about money more than any other age group, including Baby Boomers.[55] That's really surprising given that so many Baby Boomers, (whose average age was 58 at the time of a Stanford Center on Longevity survey), report having no money saved for retirement.[56] Baby Boomers hold less wealth, are deeper in debt and will face higher expenses than retirees a decade older than them, yet don't worry as much as millennials. Interesting, right? Why aren't they as worried? They believe they have more options.

"Boomers who run out of funds towards the end of life will either fall back on their children, who by then will be in their 50s and 60s, or the

---

[54] https://www.cnbc.com/2019/05/24/25-percent-of-americans-say-they-worry-about-money-all-the-time.html

[55] https://www.cnbc.com/2019/02/12/this-is-the-no-1-cause-of-stress.html

[56] https://www.cnbc.com/2018/11/07/one-third-of-baby-boomers-had-nothing-saved-for-retirement-at-age-58-.html

social safety network," said Jialu Streeter, a research scientist at Stanford.[57]

If we have regrets, or believe we have more options, we're obviously thinking about money. So why aren't more people comfortable with doing something about their financial situation? I started asking myself and others the same thing. It's one of the reasons why I wrote this book. I think America's struggle with money boils down to three things:

- **First: Education.** We don't understand how money works - in other words we're not educated enough about money. We don't understand how to budget, save, invest, or make smart money choices. We know enough to earn and spend, but the details of budgeting, saving, and investing seem to be intimidating.
- **Secondly: Mindset.** The average American mindset around money is negative or fear based. We don't see and embrace money as a tool, or as something we believe we deserve. We're uncomfortable, scared, or angry with money.
- **Thirdly: Inaction**. In spite of millions of articles, websites, experts, podcasts and books about money and learning to manage it, we avoid, delay, and resist starting now and taking action to change our situation. We procrastinate, thinking things will somehow solve themselves, or that we'll magically wake up and be money masters, able to control and wring wealth out of our situation.

I was recently reading *7 Myths That Are Killing Your Wealth Potential*, a book by Keith Weinhold. Weinhold is the Founder of GetRichEducation.com. He is also the newest contributing writer at the Rich Dad Advisors blog, and he's a young real estate investor. Something in his book really stood out to me. He wrote, "It makes no sense. People spend tons of time learning about how to work. They spend zero time learning

---

[57] https://www.cnbc.com/2018/11/07/one-third-of-baby-boomers-had-nothing-saved-for-retirement-at-age-58-.html

about how money works. Yet money is the main reason that they go to work."[58]

Life, whether we realize it or not, is one long learning process. You can live and learn, or live, not learn, and suffer. I prefer to learn. That's why I like to say that during times of financial discovery or change, including times of stress and struggle, be grateful. When we struggle or fail at something, we are given insights and opportunities for personal and financial growth and improvement. Failure is how we eventually succeed. It's up to us to learn from those times so we don't repeat the lesson or get "held back," by what we've failed to learn.

There's nothing wrong with failing and learning from our failures, but the longer we go without learning, the more regrets we'll have. There are general regrets at all ages, like "not learning more about money early in life," or "not starting to save and disciplining myself to save," or "not getting a second opinion about your money strategy" and so on. But there are other financial regrets through the ages:

Regrets People Have About Their 20s

Robert Kiyosaki is a strong proponent of learning about money early, and so am I. Too many parents, who don't know much more about money than their children, fail to teach their children about money. They rely on the school system, or "life," to do what they can't. Or, they feel uncomfortable talking about money because they don't see it as the tool it is. The regrets people have about their 20s are:

- **Not learning more about money and how the world works.** Money ignorance is a primary reason so many 20-somethings are living at home with mom and dad after they graduate from college.

---

[58] Keith Weinhold. 7 Money Myths That Are Killing Your Wealth Potential Money Secrets You Wish You Knew http://www.getricheducation.com/wp-content/uploads/2017/10/7_Money_Myths_Free_Download.pdf

- **Student loan debt.** There's nothing like a $100,000 student loan debt looming over you and your minimum wage job to stir deep regrets. The son of one of my clients was desperate to pay off his loan after college. When he couldn't find a job that paid a living wage, he joined the Navy, became a welder, and now, in his mid-30s, makes about $75,000 a year — near the top end of what Navy welders make, but almost double the $34,000 he would have made as a teacher. He doesn't regret college and his degree, but he does regret taking out a loan to do so. If he had it to do over again, he'd have saved money for college, or joined the military and let them pay for it.

- **Credit card debt.** With easy access to credit cards in college, and after graduation, it's easy to incur huge credit card debt on top of student loan debt. The debt totals can be crushing, especially if you're not making a living wage. Because debt is so often glamorized and accepted, it's hard to resist the urge to own and use credit cards.

- **Not saving for retirement.** My clients often tell me, "If I knew then what I know now," that they'd have started saving for retirement beginning with the money they got from birthday gifts, chores, allowance, and their part-time job earnings.

"I can't believe my parents didn't tell me about compounding," Richard told me. "It's such a simple concept. I had over $500 in a jar in my closet that I'd saved from odd jobs, birthday money and whatnot by the time I was 13. What if I'd had that in a bank account all that time?" Richard regrets "wasting" ten years of not putting his money into an account where it did earn interest.

"I mean, I knew I should save, and I did," he said, "But I'd have saved more if I knew about compounding."

By the time Richard was a junior in college he'd learned more about managing his money, but he still regrets the years between

8 and 18, when he didn't understand how money worked. He lived in a pre-internet age, and his parents didn't talk about money other than to tell him to save a dollar out of every ten dollars he earned. It's not a horrendous loss, but it's a loss.

- **Treating money as a status symbol rather than a financial tool.** In February 2019 financial blogger and writer Stephanie Halligan told FinanceBlog.com, "In my early 20s, I remember treating my money as a status symbol. I was earning my first 'adult' paycheck and I felt like I deserved to buy more: more clothes, more travel, more eating out."

  While Halligan's not alone in her spending behavior, I think it's one many of us don't think about. The desire to spend the money we've "rightly earned" on ourselves is universal. It's an attempt at "retail therapy," i.e. spending money in order to "feel good" about ourselves. It's a short-term fix, but it's not a solution. Halligan was able to get her spending under control, pay off $34,579 in student loan debt in four years, and create a new career for herself as a personal finance writer. She writes, coaches, and cartoons about money at empowereddollar.com and she no longer uses money as a status symbol.

Regrets People Have in Their 30s

Student loan burdens are the biggest regret Millennials have. More than 17% of those polled cited their school loans as a regret. Millennials' regret over student loans was more than twice that of Gen Xers (7%) and more than three times that of Boomers (4%). Not understanding how the financial decisions they made in their 20s would affect the rest of their lives bothers them. From investing to taking on debt, to failing to save or budget, money issues are a huge part of the regrets we have in our 30s.

- **Not saving for retirement was the number one regret of Millennials surveyed by New York Life.** Respondents pinpointed this mistake to age 34, on average, and said it took over a decade to recover.

- Fidelity recommends having at least two times your annual salary saved by age 35 and three times your salary by age 40.[59]

- **Not maintaining an emergency fund was second on the survey.** Survey respondents also said they regretted not maintaining an adequate emergency fund in their early 30s—a mistake that took an average of nine years to recover from, the survey found.[60]

- **Financial planners recommend everyone have between three- and six-months' worth of their expenses socked away in cash.** A savings account is fine, but it should preferably be in a high-yield savings or money-market account where there's potential for growth but zero risk of loss. Your emergency fund total depends on your monthly expenses and the stability of your income. For a single-earner household the total is six months, while the guideline for a dual-earner household is three months. If you freelance or are self-employed, you may need even more, up to a year in expenses.[61]

- **Credit card debt was a major regret.** The survey found that the debt respondents took on took them an average of eight years to recover from. Along with debt they also regretted not paying their balances off in full every month. If you're going to own and use credit cards and still build wealth—and earn perks and rewards—it's crucial to avoid carrying a balance. [62]

---

[59] https://www.businessinsider.com/top-money-regrets-30s-retirement-savings-credit-cards-2019-9
[60] Ibid.
[61] Ibid
[62] Ibid

I think that Tanza Loudenback, writer for *Business Insider* and her article on the top 10 mistakes people in their 30s make, are spot on.[63] But they're also applicable for all ages:

1. **Prioritizing your kid's college over your retirement.** Both are important, but if you don't have your 401K and retirement funds set up, your child may end up supporting you.[64]

2. **Saving in all the wrong places.** Some people put too much emphasis on their 401K/retirement plan and don't save for other life events — a house, car, wedding, kids. Save for retirement, but don't neglect other savings accounts that you'll need to have for other purchases.[65]

3. **Neglecting Insurance in general — health, life, home, and disability.** The Social Security Administration estimates that over 25% of today's 20-year-olds will be disabled before retirement.[66]

4. **Not talking about money while making your wedding plans.** Sure, it's important to know how your future spouse feels about kids, work, and where you'll live, but even more important is having the "money talk." This talk allows you both to understand how your future partner-for-life makes financial decisions and whether or not you want to separate finances if you're both working. If you decide to combine income, you must agree on how to spend the joint money.

5. **Spending too much money on your wedding.** Yes, we all want our wedding to be memorable and special, but that doesn't mean it has to cost the same as a healthy down payment on a house!

---

[63] https://www.businessinsider.com/worst-money-mistakes-to-make-in-your-30s-2017-6#1-saving-too-much-in-the-wrong-places-1
[64] Ibid
[65] Ibid
[66] Ibid

According to Knot (a wedding website) the average wedding to-day costs a whopping $33,931.[67]

6. **Overspending on cars.** Cars are depreciating assets. Some people insist on a new car every year or so, but the rule of thumb is to space your cars out ten years apart. Buy a new car if you must but be sure to pay it off in five years; that way, for the next five years, you can build up other savings. After 10 years, hit the dealerships again.[68]

7. **Overspending on the first child.** You don't need the most expensive strollers, cribs, and toys, but people somehow pull out all the stops on the first kid, only to regret it by the time the second one comes along. Buy the least expensive, but practical items and sock the rest away in a college fund. Trust me, your child will appreciate it so much more.

8. **Going to graduate school for the wrong reasons.** If you're going back to school, especially if you're paying for it out of your own pocket, you should have a purpose and career track for that degree.

9. **Taking short-term jobs for the money, not because they translate to helping you make more money in your 40s and 50s.** It's okay to explore career paths, or starting a business, but only because that job will help you make money down the road, not just in the short term.

10. **Not living below your means and not saving.** "Savings first" is the rule. Save for retirement first and spend with whatever is left over. Pay your future first, and then make sure your present is secure.[69]

---

[67] Ibid
[68] https://www.businessinsider.com/worst-money-mistakes-to-make-in-your-30s-2017-6#8-overspending-on-cars-8
[69] https://www.businessinsider.com/worst-money-mistakes-to-make-in-your-30s-2017-6#1-saving-too-much-in-the-wrong-places-1

Regrets People Have in Their 40s

As we get older, we regret a lot of things, from the career track we picked, not traveling enough, or spending enough time with friends, family, children and not taking care of our bodies. In our 40s our regrets about money begin to rear up. Many of us take action, but regret "waiting" so long to do so. The 40s are a time when we see the "top of the hill," coming into sight. We sometimes panic, wondering if we have waited too long to chase our dreams. We think we still have time, but we start to examine our lives. Some of the things we regret most about money in our 40s have a lot to do with time:

1. **Staying in a job too long or not starting a business when we had the chance.** People stick with a job they hate or even feel indifferent about, because of the money. They think leaving or starting over somewhere else is "too risky." Once they do finally leave, they realize they should have done it years before.
2. **Wasting time on parties, television, things that give us no return on our participation or investment.**
3. **Didn't invest sooner.** When we're young, time stretches on for what seems like an eternity. We don't invest when we're young because a part of us always believes there will always be plenty of time to do so — until there's not.
4. **Waiting to save or not saving enough.** Like investing, we think there will always be time to start "adulting" and start saving, but we don't. And then once we do, we're shocked at how those 5, 10, 15 years of compounding interest could have made us so much of the money we'll never see.
5. **Failing to budget.** Again, time and how we wasted it is one of the major regrets of those in their 40s. As time catches up with us and we start looking at retirement, health, and other issues coming up in the next decade or two, we begin to see how we wasted time.

6. **Didn't take staying healthy seriously enough.** When we're young, unless we're in an accident, get cancer, or have life related health consequences, we don't think about working to stay healthy. We take our health for granted. It's in our 40s, when our body begins to show the signs and symptoms of aging, of not being properly maintained, etc. that we begin to regret not investing more in staying healthy.

7. **Lending money.** There's just something about being able to help out friends and family with a sizeable loan to buy a car, or put a down payment on a house, or get married. If we're making money, we reason, this is the time to do it. Or is it? That $5,000 or $10,000 we loaned that we're never going to get back (there's a reason the bank told your family or friend 'no' on a loan) begins to take on real significance, especially when you calculate lost interest.

8. **Getting married** (and spending too much on the wedding!). Not everyone marries in their 20s or 30s. Many people marry later in life, or they get married for the second, third, or even fourth time — and end up regretting it.

9. **Ignoring their credit score.** The only thing many of us know about our credit score is that a high one is good, a low one is bad. Once the score drops and we can no longer buy a car, or a house, or get a loan it's only then we begin to understand the power a credit score has. And we regret ignoring it, especially once we understand the time, effort, and cost it takes to raise a score once it has fallen.

Regrets People Have in Their 50s

Who hasn't heard the term 'mid-life crisis'? Well, when you hit 50 'crises' is practically a rite of passage, beginning with a growing awareness of your life's regrets. At 40, if we haven't taken care of our bodies we start to ache and creak. By age 50 most of us have definitely noticed we're not moving as fast, as easily, or with as much energy as we did in our 30s and 40s. That's about the time we become aware of other things that aren't working so well — mostly financial things, but we also regret things like not taking more chances, or our wasting time worrying about our looks, our possessions, or what people think of us. We regret not traveling more, especially if poor health prevents it now and in the future. We really begin to regret not being more financially savvy. And finally, we regret not standing up for others or ourselves — especially when it comes to needing to make tough financial decisions.

1. **Not saying 'no' to those who want to borrow money from us, or who want us to invest in their business or ideas.** This is especially true of investing in our adult children. We want to support them, even if our business sense screams not to. True, there are some amazing investment stories out there, like when Daymond John's mother mortgaged her home to the tune of $100,000 to invest in her son's business. Daymond spent the money wisely, but he came close to losing his mother's home. With an additional $2,000 she got from her son waiting tables at Red Lobster, she was able to pull them out of the pending loss with a smart decision at the last minute. She saved both her home and her son's business.

2. **Not investing sooner.** As with most life events, it takes maturity, time, and distance to see where we went wrong. Call it Monday morning quarterbacking, regrets, or wisdom, most of us regret not investing sooner.

3. **Not saving more.** The closer we get to retirement the more it dawns on us that we didn't save enough money to retire. In fact, we realize with a shock, we may never be able to retire, and will end up working until we're carried away in a box.

4. **Wasting time.** We regret wasting time because it's only with age that we realize time is not endless. We regret wasting time because we realize we've wasted business and educational opportunities, as well as savings and investment opportunities.

5. **Not taking more risks.** I tell my younger clients to take bigger risks now, when there's time to recover. The older we get, the less time we have to come back from a big financial fail. Risks include things like exploring a career, travel, relationships, and yes—money. Start a business, invest. The older we get the more we understand how much better life might have been had we risked more in our youth.

Regrets People Have in Their 60s+

Baby Boomers have several big regrets, almost all of them around money. According to a recent AARP bulletin, baby boomers spend $7 trillion per year on goods and services. And even though they are aging (the very youngest boomers are in their late 50s as of 2019) they continue to hold corporate and economic power—80 percent of the country's personal net worth belongs to boomers. Forty-five percent of Baby Boomers have no retirement saved at all. Only 55 percent of Boomers have any money saved for retirement. Almost one-half of the 45 percent or one in five boomers, had retirement savings at some point, but no longer do.[70] One-third of baby boomers plan to retire at age 70 or older, or not at all. Six in 10 boomers have taken no action with their workplace defined contribution plans.[71] [72] Do Baby Boomers have regrets? You bet they do:

1. **Not taking enough financial risks when they're young.** The time to take financial risks, to avoid conservative retirement accounts overloaded with fixed income investments is in your 20s, 30s, and 40s. By taking risks, such as looking more at S&P 500 Index investments for instance, most of us could have increased our retirement funds by 20-30 percent. Once you lose a large

---

[70] https://www.myirionline.org/docs/default-source/default-document-library/iri_babyboomers_whitepaper_2019_final.pdf?sfvrsn=0
[71] Ibid
[72] https://www.investopedia.com/terms/b/baby_boomer.asp

sum of money during retirement, it's very difficult if not impossible to recover — so take risks while you're young.

2. **Not resisting the siren song of credit cards.** "Paying with plastic" is so common that the Federal Reserve says total U.S. credit card debt topped $1 trillion in 2017. Debt has come a long way since credit cards came into popular use in the 1950s. Credit for farmers and merchants, has been around since Biblical times, but most historians trace the modern credit card to the founding of Diners Club in 1950. The Diner's Club card was the first charge card that could be used to make purchases at multiple retailers. Generations prior to the 1950s saw debt as undesirable, but Baby Boomers who grew up with credit and credit cards saw debt, particularly credit card debt, as just part of life — not understanding how much money they would, could, and did waste in interest charges on their credit cards. According to a NerdWallet study, credit card debt costs the average U.S. household more than $2,500 in interest per year.

That $2,500 is more than 3percent of the average household income. Is that worth the privilege of carrying debt on a credit card? According to Numbeo data, it's enough to pay for two months' rent and utilities in the U.S., based on average costs.[73]

Doesn't seem like much? Multiply that by 10 years = $25,000. Or times 40 years, the life of the average Baby Boomer's use of credit cards and it averages $100,000. Now, imagine that $100,000 being in the bank, or compounded interest on that $2,500 a year for 40 years. That's one big regret.

3. **Not planning for retirement.** What many people don't realize is that retirement has always been part of a plan to get older

---

[73] https://www.nerdwallet.com/blog/credit-cards/stop-wasting-money-on-credit-card-interest/

adults out of the workforce so younger (cheaper to hire), and more productive workers could replace them. Retiring from a company meant getting half of your pay (which was deducted from a new worker), plus social service money (Social Security, Medicaid/Medicare) and any funds you saved so you could leave the workforce and pursue more leisurely things. While companies used to offer good pension plans, over the years most companies have done away with pensions in favor of the 401K. A 401K is a plan which the employee must contribute to if they hope for any sort of retirement.[74] Not understanding their 401K and not paying the maximum allowed into it is a major regret for many Baby Boomers.

4. **Not saving enough.** Saving is simple, but so many of us fail to take it seriously. We claim we "don't make enough" to save any substantial amounts. My clients laugh when I explain that even $100 to $300 a month can make a big dent in their retirement in five, ten, or forty years. For those in their 60s this truth finally becomes evident when they realize they haven't saved enough.

5. **Withdrawing money from retirement accounts.** It may not seem like much to withdraw money periodically from your retirement account to buy a new car, make a down payment on a house, or pay for your, or your kid's college, or wedding, but it can really tear up your retirement down the road. Even if you cash out your 401K when changing jobs other than rolling it over, you can suffer financial consequences like having to pay income tax beyond the possible 10% early withdrawal fees prior to age 59 ½.

6. **Postponing an estate plan or making a will.** Let's face it, no one likes to think about dying. [75] So, it's no surprise that more than half of Americans don't have a will, and even fewer have

---

[74] https://www.seattletimes.com/nation-world/a-brief-history-of-retirement-its-a-modern-idea/

[75] https://www.fidelity.com/viewpoints/personal-finance/do-you-need-an-estate-plan

an estate plan. What's the difference? A will is (or can be) a relatively simple document that sets forth your wishes regarding the distribution of property. If you have minor children, your will may also include instructions regarding their care. A true estate plan which utilizes Living Trusts and Irrevocable Trusts does so much more than a simple will. It directs the distribution of assets and legacy wishes, but more importantly it helps you and your heirs have estate privacy, potentially pay substantially less in taxes, fees, and court costs. You should always consult a legal and/or tax advisor to discuss your unique situation to determine what may be the best approach for you. Make sure the attorney is well versed in designing and the full implementation of trusts. But don't wait to act. Act now.

7. **Living as long as they have without financial planning of any kind.**

    Baby Boomers, for the most part, have finally seen their children launch, and have downsized their large homes for smaller homes or condos. They're finished paying for their child's college, and they're no longer chauffeuring their children places — although many do play Uber for their grandchildren. They're not spending what they did in their 30s, 40s and even 50s. They finally have enough time to look at retirement and their financial situation, and they're not liking what they see. Like I pointed out above, 45 percent of them have no retirement savings at all, and most of the 55 percent who do, don't have enough.

"I could kick myself for not starting to save for my retirement earlier," Dave told me.

He and his wife, both 63 and considering retirement, were devastated to discover they would probably both need to keep working at least part time for another seven to ten years if they wanted to maintain the lifestyle they were living now. They didn't have an extravagant life, but it was comfortable, and they wanted it to remain that way.

"Is it too late to start saving and planning?" he asked me.

"It's never too late," I told him. And while that's true, the hard facts are that even with the magic of compounding there is just no way to catch up with the amount Dave could have had if he'd started saving sooner. Experts suggest saving a minimum of $250,000, and preferably closer to $500,000 or a million for retirement. Baby Boomers like Dave, who start saving later in life, assume they'll just work longer to make up the difference. What they fail to take into account is their age, health problems, the power of compounding interest over half a century rather than 5-to-10 years, and whether or not they'll be able to find or keep the employment they have well into their 60s or 70s. Ageism is still a thing and many of my clients find themselves being encouraged (pushed out) to retire to make room for younger, less expensive workers. It can be a shock to lose a job, and not have much money saved for retirement.

"I wish we hadn't pulled money from our IRA for Joanie's wedding," he said. I nodded.

"You're not alone. One of the most common financial mistakes people make is withdrawing money early from their savings or IRA. The extra taxes and penalties, plus lost benefits just aren't worth giving up your financial future just to borrow a small sum now," I said.

"I know. It's just that she's our only daughter and she's been such a good kid, and we just wanted to make her wedding special," he said. "How special was it?" I asked.

"$20,000 special," he said. "Ouch." "Yeah, but it could have been worse," he laughed.

It could have. The average cost of a wedding varies, but the website costofwedding.com says the national average is $25,764. Another site, The Knot, reports an average cost of a wedding for 100-150 guests is about $33,391.

"And we pitched in another $10,000, with the groom's parents, to give them $20,000 for a down payment on a house." I winced.

I know it's tempting to make sure your kid's have a great wedding, but that money could have been spent paying down student debt or investing in real estate their kids could rent to own from them. What Dave didn't know was that according to the CDC, he and his wife both had at least another 20 years to live, 20 years they'd both either relish or regret, depending on the lifestyle they were willing to adopt to make it financially.

The CDC states that the average American male will live to the age of 81.6. Females can expect an average lifespan of 84.5 years. It's simple math. If Dave and his wife retired at age 63 or even 65, they'd still need enough money saved, or an income that would last another 18-20 years. The CDC average is not the worst-case scenario. Dave and his wife were both healthy, active and could live even longer. Or, they could both have health issues and the added burden of medical bills, hospital stays, or treatment for cancers, diabetes, and other diseases that come with age.

SUMMARY

There are regrets for every stage of life. It's up to you to figure out how old you'll be before you wake up and realize that if you want a solid, comfortable retirement at an age you decide, then you need to start planning now, no matter what your age. The most common regrets I see day after day are:

1. Waiting too long to get your money, spending, budget, and savings under control.
2. Failing to learn all you can about your money, how it works, and how to use it as a tool to create the life you want to live now, and in the future.
3. Not taking money seriously. As long as people have a 'good job' and a comfortable income they don't take money seriously. They only get motivated once they lose the good job, and the income,

and start experiencing health, life, or financial challenges—when it's not impossible, but certainly much harder to manage.

4. Waiting to act on any or all phases of their financial life. No matter how old you are right now, reread all the regrets from each stage of life and think about where you are now. What do you need to be doing to ensure your retirement is not lived out in poverty, substandard housing or where you work until you die?

5. Failing to get that "Second Opinion" about ways to maximize their savings and compounding efforts. Considering ways to increase their after-tax returns, lowering interest rates on credit lines, and to never again feel like just a "number" with their current advisor. Second opinions are what everyone orders when it comes to your health or chronic medical conditions. Why not for your Financial Well Being as well? This will apply to any economic or market cycle as well as any interest rate environment.

CHAPTER NINE
AVOIDING SCAMS & FINANCIAL BUBBLE'S

"Greed is not an investment Strategy." ~ Jay Kemmerer

Frank Abagnale isn't on my official list of financial experts, but he probably should be. If you're not familiar with Frank, he's one of the most famous scam artists in history, and his story, depicted in his memoir, and later in the movie, *Catch Me if You Can*, is about Frank's legendary financial frauds and scams as a teenager in the 1960s.

While still under the legal drinking age in the states where he ran his schemes, Frank successfully posed as an airline pilot, a doctor and a lawyer and more. He collected and cashed legitimate and illegitimate paychecks, passed hundreds of thousands of dollars of bad checks, flew for free, practiced medicine, and lived the high life before finally being caught.

For years Frank exploited America's fascination and faith in the physical symbols and trappings of success. By simply wearing the right clothes, saying the right words and flashing the right status symbols, Frank was able to be whomever he wanted — doctor, lawyer, and executive. "People only know what you tell them," he explained in interviews later. The people who believed what he told them fell head over heels into his stories.[76]

Frank now works with law enforcement and corporations and gives talks to tell people how to avoid scams. His number one piece of advice? Never use a debit card. Always use a credit card. It's 180 degrees difference from what Dave Ramsey says. Ramsey says "Don't even own a credit card. Only use a debit card." But Frank's advice is coming from a security standpoint. Ramsey is looking at a spending and discipline angle.

Frank points out that when there's another large data breach (they're almost like major holidays, they come around every few months) and a criminal gets your credit card number and charges $1 million on it, you're protected. Not only are you protected, your credit card company will cancel the card, and send you a new one in 3-10 days. You won't be responsible for charges any criminal makes either. Not so with a debit card. With a debit card you'll lose everything in your account and then some, plus charges.

Also, Abagnale says, keep your check-writing to a minimum and be vigilant about examining your bank statements frequently.[77]

Every year, millions of American consumers—nearly 7 percent of the population—are victims of scams and fraud. Most scammers are not nearly as brilliant or creative as Frank Abagnale, but their efforts are still costly. In 2017, the number of fraud victims in the US reached 16.7 million, with $16.8 billion lost.[78]

Money may be a game, but it's not one you can play while distracted or unfocused. All money errors aren't due to fraud. You can also lose

---

[76] https://www.nytimes.com/watching/titles/catch-me-if-you-can
[77] https://www.nytimes.com/watching/titles/catch-me-if-you-can
[78] https://www.nytimes.com/watching/titles/catch-me-if-you-can

money, get fined, or run afoul of the law if you don't pay attention to your investments, spending, or decisions.

Even the pros aren't immune to fraud or making uninformed decisions. Warren Buffet recounts several instances where he hasn't done his due diligence.

In 2011, Warren Buffett and Berkshire Hathaway caught a lot of legal heat when David Sokal pitched Lubrizol Corp. to Buffett as a potential takeover company. The problem was that Sokol owned stock in the chemicals company.

Berkshire bought the company and Sokol earned a $3 million profit on the deal. Sounds pretty sweet, right? However, Sokal hadn't told Buffett he owned stock in Lubrizol, and that violated insider-trading rules. Buffett didn't realize his mistake immediately, but later admitted at a stockholder's meeting that he should have probed deeper with Sokol.

Buffett says the investment advice to follow here is not to be overly trusting of anyone or anything, no matter how well you think you know the situation or the person. Ask more questions than you think are necessary, because you can't be too careful when your money is on the line.

Don't be afraid to ask the hard questions. There is no offensive or stupid question if you're seeking more information. If you get a gut feeling something is wrong, then it probably is. Don't hesitate to walk away from what appears to be a great investment, but just doesn't feel right. You don't have to be able to prove or explain your decision. Just trust your gut.

IT'S NOT JUST BIG INVESTMENTS THAT SCAM YOU

While it's the big or historic scams that get national financial media attention, you can fall prey to a variety of smaller financial and investment scams as well:

Airbnb and House/Vacation Property Rental Scams

With the prospect of making big money fast on rental property, housing and vacation rentals, a lot of legitimate homeowners are renting their property out and making good money. Where there is legitimate money to be made, there's also illegitimate money to be made. Scam artists have made this new rental trend their new scam. Posing on sites like Airbnb, Craigslist, and Facebook's Marketplace, they advertise fictitious properties for rent. They snare victims by posting attractive pictures and detailed information on the property.

The suggested rental price for the property will be well below the current market, which is how they attract their victims. They will only converse with prospective renters via a VOIP (computer) phone number that's located in a foreign country. After an agreement is in place, the down payment or rental payment must be made through a money transfer process.

You send your payment, but when you go to check in, no one has heard of you, or you're misdirected to another property that is nothing like the one you signed up for, or worse, there is no property. And good luck getting your money back if you've gone through Airbnb. Airbnb doesn't have a system in place to stop scammers, even though they're getting significant backlash from the growing number of scammers using their site. The Washington Post, Vice.com and other media outlets continue to warn renters about rental scams. *The Washington Post* even detailed a $12,000 scam that happened on Airbnb.

While scammers target anyone with money, financial scams targeting seniors are growing. In fact, they're considered by many law enforcement agencies to be the top crime of the 21st century. Scammers believe that Baby Boomers have significant money sitting around in personal accounts and aren't very financially savvy. Often, they are looking for ways to make up for the retirement they didn't plan for — so they make good targets.

Financial scams can be difficult to prosecute, and many of those who find out they've been scammed are ashamed, and reluctant to report the scam, so financial scams are considered a "low-risk" crime. While the low risk benefits the scammer, the financial loss is often devastating to many older adults. It can leave them vulnerable, unprotected and unable to recoup their losses.

Other popular targets for scammers include low-income adults. Sadly, these scams usually come from family members! Over 90 percent of all reported elder abuse is committed by an older person's own family members, most often their adult children, followed by grandchildren, nieces and nephews, and others.

The National Council on Aging's list of popular investment and financial scams against seniors:

Medicare/health insurance scams

Because all U.S. citizens or permanent residents over age 65 qualify for Medicare, there is rarely any need for a scam artist to research what private health insurance company older people have in order to take them for some money.

This scam involves perpetrators posing as a Medicare representative to get older people to give them their personal information. They may also set up bogus kiosks in malls, or at makeshift mobile clinics. They'll use the information on the form they give you to fill out, then use the personal information they provide to bill Medicare and pocket the money. You're rarely the wiser.

Counterfeit Prescription Drugs

Seniors are turning to the internet for more and more services, including buying specialized medication. This scam has been growing in popularity for the last 20 years and doesn't appear to be going away. The FDA has investigated an average of 20 cases per year, up from five a year in the 1990s.

This scam is dangerous for both your wallet as well as your health. You're not only spending money for a substance that won't help your medical condition, you may be buying a substance that can inflict even more harm.

Funeral & Cemetery Scams

The FBI warns about two types of funeral and cemetery fraud they're seeing.

In one fraud, scammers search obituaries and then call or attend a complete stranger's funeral in order to take advantage of the grieving widow or widower. They will claim the deceased had an outstanding debt with them and will try to extort money from relatives to settle the fake debts.

Disreputable funeral homes will often attempt to capitalize on family members' unfamiliarity with the cost of funeral services. Funeral directors will add unnecessary charges to the bill, often insisting that a casket, usually the most expensive part of funeral services, is necessary. The fact is, even a direct cremation, can be accomplished with a cardboard casket in place of an expensive display or burial casket.

Fraudulent anti-aging products

Who doesn't want to look their best, even as they age? More and more people, men and women, feel the need to conceal their age in order to get hired, or to participate in social media. It's a vanity that causes them to look for new treatments and medications to maintain a youthful appearance. These treatments may be fake Botox—like the one in 2006 in Arizona that netted its distributors $1.5 million in less than a year. Even legitimate Botox is dangerous. The root ingredient, botulism neuro-toxin, is one of the most toxic substances known to science. Imagine the damage the fake stuff, or a bad batch can do. If you've been in any pharmacy, grocery store, or vitamin store you've seen or bought completely bogus homeopathic remedies that do absolutely nothing.

Telemarketing/phone scams

As a group, seniors make twice as many purchases over the phone than the national average. They're not just lonely and wanting to talk, they're also far more familiar and trusting with shopping over the phone.

In the absence of any face-to-face interaction or a paper trail, these scams are incredibly hard to trace. Once a person falls victim to one scam their name is often shared with other scammers looking for easy targets. Sometimes the same person can be scammed repeatedly. Simply thinking through an opportunity, asking questions, and not being seduced by greed can protect most victims.

Examples of telemarketing fraud include:

The Pigeon Drop

The con artist informs their target that she/he found a large sum of money and is willing to split it if the person will make a "good faith" payment by withdrawing funds from his/her bank account. A second con artist is frequently involved, posing as a lawyer, banker, or some other credible, trustworthy stranger.

The Fake Accident Ploy

We have social media to thank for this popular ploy. The con artist convinces the victim to wire transfer or send money using the pretext that the person's child or another relative is in the hospital and needs the money.

Charity Scams

If you've ever heard or read about a local or national tragedy, chances are you've been moved to want to help, either by donating money to a GoFundMe or other social giving account. Be careful. Money is often solicited for fake charities, natural disasters, and bogus illnesses.

Internet Fraud

Not all of us are internet geniuses. Many of us can't tell when a website is secure, or if a pop-up ad or warning is legitimate or not. Older users, as well as those just adopting the internet, are more trusting than those who have used the net for years. Based upon the naivete of those seniors or internet neophytes, pop-up browser windows simulating virus-scanning software will fool victims into either downloading a fake anti-virus program (at a substantial cost), or it's an actual virus that accesses whatever information is on the user's computer and reveals it to scammers.

Seniors' lack of familiarity with the more unknown aspects of browsing the web (i.e., firewalls and built-in virus protection) make them especially susceptible to such traps. But, anyone can fall victim to social engineering and other internet scams like:

Email/phishing Scams

The victim receives email messages that appear to be from a legitimate company or institution, like the IRS. This email may ask them to update their password or verify their personal information to receive a refund.

Investment Schemes

Once you start thinking about and planning for retirement, you'll be amazed at the number of schemes targeting you for your money. Many are aimed at seniors, but anyone can fall victim to them.

From pyramid schemes like Madoff's (which included a number of senior citizens among its victims) all the way down the line to fables of a Nigerian prince looking for a partner to claim inheritance money, the stories and scams are complex and believable. They may range from the simple to complex financial products that many economists don't even understand. Investment scams are a popular and easy way to take advantage of anyone of any age. Buyer beware.

Homeowner/reverse Mortgage Scams

If you're one of the few to own your home outright, beware. Scammers like to take advantage of that fact. Because many people above a certain age own their homes, they become a very specific target.

For instance, in San Diego a particularly elaborate property tax scam saw fraudsters sending mailers to homeowners offering property tax assessment reduction in return for hundreds of dollars in fees.

California's Attorney General Edmund G. Brown pointed out that property tax reassessment is offered for free by county tax assessors. Should a homeowner believe they are overpaying in property taxes due to the decline in value of their home, they should call their local tax assessor for a free reassessment, Brown said. The letters were apparently sent on behalf of the County Assessor's Office. The letter was made to look official but displayed only public information. It would identify the property's assessed value then offer the homeowner, for a fee of course, to arrange for a reassessment of the property's value and therefore the tax burden associated with it.

Property is a popular target for scammers. Along with tax assessment fraud, there is the potential for a reverse mortgage borrower to be scammed. A reverse mortgage can be legit, but those considering them should be wary of people in their lives pressuring them to obtain a reverse mortgage, especially if they stand to benefit from the borrower accessing equity, such as home repair companies, family, and those who approach the older adult directly.

Sweepstakes & Lottery Scams

Everyone likes to 'win' money, be it through the lottery, or a contest. Scammers take advantage of this and inform their victim they've won a lottery or sweepstakes of some kind. The catch is the 'winner' will need to make a payment of some kind to get their prize. Or, they'll simply be sent a check saying, 'You've won!' They can deposit the very real looking check into their bank account and even see it show up in their new balance immediately. It will take 3-10 days before the fake check is rejected. During that time the scammers collect their money for the fees or taxes on the prize and then disappear. As soon as the fake check is rejected, the winner is left with the fees and taxes taken from their account and no way to recoup their losses.

The Grandparent Scam

The grandparent scam preys on the compassion and love of grandparents love of their grandchildren. Scammers will call an older person, then say something along the lines of "Hi Grandma, do you know who this is?" The unsuspecting grandparent guesses the name of the grandchild the scammer most sounds like. This gives the scammer an "in," if they can then convince the grandparent they are indeed that adult child.

Once they've convinced their grandparent of their identity, the fake grandchild will ask for money to solve some unexpected financial problem (overdue rent, payment for car repairs, etc.), to be paid through

Western Union or MoneyGram, which don't always require identification to collect. They'll also beg the scammed grandparent not to tell their parents, which is how the scammer often avoids being revealed.

HISTORY DOES REPEAT ITSELF

There are dozens, if not hundreds of investment scams throughout history. Surprisingly, many of these scams were created and implemented by teenagers! Scams all share two things in common. They rely on people's trust, and reluctance, or inability, to ask hard questions about what they're investing in, and on people's greed. Investopedia lists the following as some of the top scams of all time:

BERNIE MADOFF

One of the most fascinating, and scariest aspects of these fraudsters is how incredibly unfazed they are by their thefts and scams. Bernie Madoff for instance, has no remorse for his Ponzi scam and blames his victims for being so stupid as to fall for it. The man who ran a Ponzi scheme of more than $60 billion has held six or seven different jobs in prison and now makes $170 a month.

On the five-year anniversary of his conviction Madoff told *Wall Street Journal* reporter Sital Patel that the people he conned "should have known better, that they didn't ask good questions about investing." He called Harry Markopolos, the fraud investigator and whistleblower who reported Madoff to the Securities and Exchange commission for his schemes, an "idiot," and reminisced fondly about his days as a financial power player.

Perhaps, more than anything else Madoff has said, his comment that people "should have known better, that they didn't ask good questions about investing," is the one truthful thing he's ever said. Indeed, it's the number one reason so many people fall victim to frauds and schemes.

We're too trusting, too believing. Like Frank Abagnale said, "People only know what you tell them."

I would add that the greed allure of making 18% on your money was the first promise made to clients by Bernie Madoff and people were seeing on their statements a gain of 1.5% per month. If you asked Bernie too many in depth questions on how he was managing the money for those consistent returns he simply would not allow you to invest with him. He kept his scam going by preying on naive investors and fooling the regulators.

It was only toward the end of his scam he reduced that interest to 12%. I know this because numerous individuals in my hometown were investing with him through what was later identified as "Feeder Funds". These were investment advisor groups, CPA Advisor Firms that had a selling agreement with him in which they earned fees for soliciting his program. I knew of only a few people who actually were lucky enough and pulled their money before the scam collapsed.

Don't be fooled. Once again, "If it sounds too good to be true, it probably is."

ZZZZ BEST CARPET CLEANING

Frank Abagnale was a teen when he pulled off his impersonations, but so was Barry Minkow, the owner and founder of ZZZZ Best Carpet Cleaning in 1986. Minkow claimed that his carpet cleaning company would become the "General Motors of carpet cleaning."

The multi-million-dollar corporation he was building wasn't based on hard work and success, but on forgery and theft. He created more than 10,000 phony documents and sales receipts without anyone suspecting a thing. His business was a complete fraud. Yet, he managed to go public and reach a market capitalization of more than $200 million—as a teenager. In his heyday he was even a featured guest on Oprah Winfrey's

TV show. He was caught and sentenced to 25 years in prison. Wow. What if he'd applied that genius to legitimate entrepreneurship?

THE SAVINGS & LOAN SCANDALS OF THE 80s

Charles Keating is another name reader's over the age of 40 will remember. Keating is the most well-known of the fraudsters who ran Savings and Loan institutions in the 80s. These companies essentially operated just like banks, but without the regulations. Without regulations, the loan institutions made what appeared to be a series of bad investments. The investments were bad for their members but enriched the corporate officers. Keating and his executives never told their investors that they were investing in worthless junk.

But you can't hide criminal activity for long. Eventually Keating was investigated, tried, and convicted of securities fraud. As a result, government regulation was promptly tightened. It was later "loosened" as the U.S. Government is heavily involved in banking and the Savings and Loan industry. In fact, five senators, including John McCain, were implicated for providing political cover to Keating and his cronies.[79]

Keating wasn't the only Savings and Loan fraudster. When the industry was deregulated under the Reagan/Bush administration, restrictions were eased on the industry. The abuse and misuse of funds that followed became easy, rampant, and went unchecked. Perhaps the most famous Savings and Loan family implicated in fraud has been the Bush family. There are other politicians that are still in office and who are still part of the Bush Jr. administration today. Jeb Bush, George Bush Sr., and his son Neil Bush have all been implicated in the Savings and Loan Scandal, which cost American taxpayers over $1.4 TRILLION dollars (note that this is about one quarter of our national debt).

---

[79] https://www.cbsnews.com/media/top-14-financial-frauds-of-all-time/

Neil Bush was the most widely targeted member of the Bush family by the press in the S&L scandal. Neil became director of Silverado Savings and Loan at the age of 30 in 1985. Three years later the institution was belly up at a cost of $1.6 billion to taxpayers to bail out.[80]

THE GREAT INSIDER TRADING SCAM

Does the name Ivan Boesky ring a bell? It should. He's the real-life trader that prototype Gordon Gecko from the movie *Wall Street*, was based on. In the 80s Boesky amassed a fortune of more than $200 million by betting on corporate takeovers, many of which occurred only a few days before the announcement of the acquisition. He was eventually charged with insider trading, cooperated with the SEC, and ultimately received a negotiated sentence of three and a half years, only serving two. He was fined a fraction of the money he made ($100 million), and permanently banned from working in the securities trade.

CENTENNIAL TECHNOLOGIES 1996.

In December 1996, Centennial Technologies recorded that the company made $2 million in revenue from PC memory cards. However, the company actually shipped fruit baskets to customers. Emanuel Pinez, the CEO of Centennial, and his employees created fake documents as evidence that they were recording sales. The price of Centennial's stock jetted up 451% to $55.50 per share on the New York Stock Exchange (NYSE).

Those numbers wouldn't last long. The Securities and Exchange Commission (SEC) reported that from April 1994 to December 1996, Centennial overstated its earnings by approximately $40 million. The company reported profits of $12 million when it had actually lost approxi-

---

[80] http://www.rationalrevolution.net/war/bush_family_and_the_s.htm

mately $28 million. The stock plunged to less than $3. Over 20,000 investors lost almost all of their investment in a company that was once considered a sure thing on Wall Street.

BRE-X MINERALS, 1997

It's not just Americans who are taken in by investment fraud. Bre-X minerals, a Canadian company, was involved in one of the largest stock swindles in history. Its Indonesian gold property, (falsely) reported to contain more than 200 million ounces, was touted to be the richest goldmine, ever. Bre-X's stock price catapulted to a high of $280 (split-adjusted), making millionaires out of ordinary people overnight. Bre-X's top value had a market capitalization of $4.4 billion. But then the goldmine was proven to be a fraud and the stock crashed. The biggest losers included the Quebec public sector pension fund, which lost $70 million, the Ontario Teachers' Pension Plan, which lost $100 million, and the Ontario Municipal Employees' Retirement Board, which lost $45 million.

ENRON, 2001

Based on their revenue alone, Enron, a Houston-based energy trading company was the seventh-largest energy company in the United States. Their secret? Accounting fraud. By using complex accounting practices, including shell companies, fictitious revenues, recording one dollar of revenue multiple times, etc. Enron was able to keep hundreds of millions worth of debt off of its books. They fooled investors and analysts into thinking the company was more fundamentally stable than it actually was.

As frauds and schemes always do, Enron's complex web of deceit unraveled and stock prices fell fast and hard, from $90 to less than 70 cents on the share. It wasn't just Enron that crashed. They took down their accounting and auditing company, Arthur Andersen, too. Arthur Andersen was the fifth leading accounting firm in the world at the time.

WORLDCOM, 2002

You'd think that the Enron scandal and subsequent convictions would have caused companies to at least hesitate before initiating their own frauds. Not so. Shortly after Enron collapsed there was another billion-dollar scandal by Telecommunications giant WorldCom. Like Enron, they too were "cooking their books," and recording operating expenses like office pens, paper, and pencils as an "investment in the company's future." Therefore, they expensed (or capitalized) the cost of these items over a number of years to the tune of $3.8 billion worth of normal operating expenses. These expenses were treated as investments and were recorded over a number of years.

In 2001, WorldCom reported profits of around $1.3 billion when in fact they were becoming increasingly unprofitable. Ultimately, tens of thousands of employees lost their jobs and investors watched their WorldCom stock fall from more than $60 to less than 20 cents per share.

TYCO INTERNATIONAL, 2002

Sometimes even the most trusted stocks and companies can be frauds. As CEO of Tyco, Dennis Kozlowski was reported to be one of the top 25 corporate managers by *BusinessWeek*. He siphoned hordes of money from Tyco, in the form of unapproved loans and fraudulent stock sales.

As a manufacturer of electronic components, safety equipment and healthcare items, Tyco was considered a safe blue-chip investment. But, with power, access and control of fortunes comes hubris, greed and fraud. Kozlowski, CFO Mark Swartz and CLO Mark Belnick received $170 million in low-to-no interest loans without shareholder approval. Kozlowski and Belnick engineered a scheme to sell 7.5 million shares of unauthorized Tyco stock for a reported $450 million. The funds were smuggled out of the company disguised as executive bonuses or bene-fits. The scandal slowly began to unravel in 2002 and Tyco's share price plummeted nearly 80% in a six-week period. A mistrial bought the ex-ecutives some time, but they were all eventually convicted and sen-tenced to 25 years in jail.

HEALTHSOUTH, 2003

"You might say wow, what a success story. Two guys start a company with no real money, and it becomes a Fortune 500 company in less than 10 years. What could go wrong?" said Aaron Beam, HealthSouth Co-founder and CFO from January 1984 through September 1997.

Apparently, plenty can go wrong. The infamous $2.8 billion accounting scandal of 2003 is proof that when executives want to falsify earnings reports, it's hard to catch them.

In the late 1990s, CEO and HealthSouth founder Richard Scrushy began instructing employees to inflate revenues and overstate HealthSouth's net income. At the time, HealthSouth was one of America's largest health care service providers. When you're one of the leaders, who's going to question you? No one, Scrushy thought — reportedly selling HealthSouth shares worth $75 million prior to releasing an earnings loss.

Beam reported that Scrushy was especially greedy, frequently stating that he wanted to be a billionaire and the richest man in Alabama.

An independent law firm concluded the sale was not directly related to the loss, and investors should have heeded the warning (they didn't ask enough questions). The Securities and Exchange Commission took note and announced that HealthSouth exaggerated revenues by $1.4 billion. The fraud was discovered when the FBI, working with HealthSouth CFO William Owens, secretly taped Scrushy discussing the fraud. Shockingly, Scrushy was acquitted of 36 counts of fraud in the case! He was however, found guilty of bribery. Scrushy arranged political contributions of $500,000, which allowed him to ensure a seat on the hospital regulatory board.

After reading all these stories, if you decided you never wanted to invest in stock again, I wouldn't blame you. Who do you trust? If you barely understand how the stock market works to begin with, I imagine these stories do nothing to reassure you. But the fact is, millions of people who didn't know what was going on with many of these companies choose not to invest because something "didn't feel quite right." Why didn't it feel quite right? Because they had educated themselves, or they knew enough to know how a legitimate company is run and they knew these companies weren't showing the signs or behavior of a legitimate company.

HOW TO AVOID SCAMS

How do you avoid scams? You educate yourself. You don't invest in things you don't understand. You ask a lot of hard questions. You don't trust everything without verifying. You do your due diligence. You check with trusted financial advisors, and you always invest with care. Most importantly, you diversify, diversify, diversify. Maintaining a well-diversified portfolio will ensure that even the best scams, if you miss the warning signs and invest anyway, don't run you off the road. They may create a lot of bumps on your road to financial independence, but they won't put you in a ditch for good.

Pump and Dump

If you've heard the term "fake news," you know how confusing it can be to know what's real, and what's false even when once trusted media are reporting the so-called facts. The same, and worse, happens in the stock market and with investments. It begins with a scheme known as pump and dump.

A company or "boiler room" of "investors," begin promoting a particular stock by any means possible—the company's website, online investment newsletters, chat rooms, email, text messages, phone calls and fax—to potential investors. From the website to promotional materials, phone calls and texts, all materials talk about how well the company is doing. These stories and materials may even tie into a real event such as new product or higher earnings, but they add false information to make the stock sound even better than it is. It's what investors want to hear, and rarely check. Remember what Frank Abagnale said, "People only know what you tell them."

These campaign pushes and positive media stimulates interest from investors who buy the stock and drive up the price. Then the people who started it all sell their shares and stop promoting the stock. This of course drives the price back down again. If new investors want to sell, they generally have to do so at a much lower price.

Pyramid Scheme

Pyramid schemes are a lot like Ponzi schemes, except instead of a central company at the center of the operation, existing investors (often unaware of the scheme) recruit new people into the scheme. In many pyramid schemes, "investors" make more from recruiting new members than they do from investing. Just like Ponzi schemes, investments are used to pay off the early investors until finally the whole scheme collapses, and most of the investors lose money. Popular pyramid schemes often involve supplements and health or beauty products.

Affinity Fraud

Are you a veteran? A cancer survivor? African American? A senior? A law enforcement officer or member of the US Military? If so, beware of affinity frauds. This type of fraud targets members of a particular group or organization — usually people with an affiliation, identity or part of a minority.

The person offering the deal either belongs to the group they're claiming to help, or they say they do. They often speak the language, use the same buzz words or slang. This helps them appear to be a trusted member of the group. Group members trust those they feel a shared bond with and may let down their guard more easily — which is what these fraudsters are relying on. The group members believe the investment is legitimate or that the return claims are realistic. Affinity fraud can involve virtually any investment, sale, or membership fee or product, including stock.

Advance Fee Fraud

One of the simplest frauds, advance fee frauds are common and easy to be taken in by. Let's say you own an investment that has been performing poorly. You want to sell it already, so you're primed to jump on this without thinking much about it. Someone contacts you with an offer to buy your investment at a price you didn't think you'd be able to get. Just send them an advance fee for their time and effort for selling your investment and you're free of your poor performing stock—only you aren't. Once you send the money, you never hear from them again. And naturally, nobody buys your shares.

Internet and Social Media Fraud

This type of fraud involves spreading false or misleading "good news" about a particular stock using the tools available online such as websites, social media posts, chat rooms, text messages and emails. The goal is to increase the price of the stock so the originator of the disinformation campaign can sell their shares at a high price. Once that happens and the campaign stops, the stock price is likely to fall (and may fall fast).

Microcap Fraud

Microcap companies have few assets and lots of low-priced shares that trade at low volumes. Scammers buy shares at a low price, then use a variety of ways to raise people's interest in the stock so the price increases. Then they sell the stock and stop promoting it. Once the promotion drops, so does the value and you're left holding essentially worthless stock. The good news is the Securities and Exchange Commission (SEC) frequently suspends trading in these stocks before they can become fraud targets. Do your due diligence and ask questions. Don't jump on a purchase before you understand it.

Pre-IPO investment scam

Greed is another guaranteed tool in the fraudster's toolbox. Who doesn't want to get in on the ground floor of another Amazon, Apple, or Microsoft? Greed and a hope of fast, big money drives many investors who are so focused on getting in on the ground floor of a potentially lucrative investment opportunity (especially an IPO or initial public offering of a stock). This type of scam offers investors a chance to buy so-called hot stocks ahead of the IPO. While there are legitimate offers to buy shares before an IPO, unregistered offerings may violate federal securities laws unless they meet a so-called registration exemption by only being offered to investors who meet income and net worth requirements.

Given the huge interest in owning IPO shares, this is a good time for you to ask "why me" in terms of why you're being offered this "amazing" opportunity instead of literally thousands of other investors. Do you know someone at the company? Or were you just a name they found in the phone book?

Offshore Scams

Not every fraud originates on American soil. There are scams outside the country that target American investors. They can involve any of the scams described above. How do they get by with it? They use something called a Regulation S, which says U.S. companies don't have to register securities with the SEC if they are sold exclusively outside of the country to offshore or foreign investors. The companies running offshore scams violate the rule and resell Regulation S stocks to U.S. investors. Because they're outside the country it's very hard for the U.S. to prosecute them, or to get your money back. Buyer beware.

TIPS FOR AVOIDING BEING SCAMMED

Five tips to avoid potential stock scams

On the one hand, the internet has made it easier than ever to spread stock scams around the world. On the other hand, it has also made it easier for the average investor to research potential stock deals and verify the legitimacy of investments. Like I said at the beginning of this chapter, greed and the failure to do your due diligence and ask hard questions is why most people fall victim to frauds and scams. When you know how things are supposed to work, and what a true return on your investment is, you're less likely to fall for a scam. Don't let greed, or your desire to make fast money, blind you to a fraudster. They're counting on your greed and the pressure they put on you, to force you into a bad decision. Once again, you're wise to remember the old adage, "If it sounds too good to be true, it's probably is."

I believe highly successful people make smaller and fewer mistakes than their neighbors, peers or their competitors, but they still make mistakes. Even Warren Buffet, as we've seen can make mistakes. Fortunately, he makes impeccable decisions too. That's how we learn. Based on this fact, people should educate themselves on what a legitimate investment is, and what an illegitimate investment is.

Having a good understanding of how scams develop, how they are marketed, how the pyramid is promoted—can help you avoid the next one that's coming your way. It might be another real estate bubble, or digital currencies like Bitcoin. Even Facebook is coming out with their own investment opportunities. What we've learned from the best scammers and fraudsters in the world is that people get caught up in scams and schemes because they're trusting, they take things at face value, they don't ask hard questions, and they don't want to offend anyone by doubting or distrusting them.

No one wants to be or look foolish. Even if they've been scammed, most people will keep it to themselves. Money is a touchier subject than sex, and losing money is even more forbidden to talk about. But it's important to learn all you can, especially if you can learn from those who were tricked. They can often offer advice you won't find online or in articles. But if you can't talk to someone who has been scammed the next best things you can do:

EDUCATE YOURSELF

> *"Risk comes from not knowing what you are doing."*
> ~ Warren Buffett

The more you know about how investing really works, and the more aware you are of common scams, the easier it will be to spot the fraud that finds its way to your inbox or mailbox. Get online. Read articles, blogs, and news stories about scams. Join an investor club, or talk to other investors. Keep up to date on the latest scams:

DON'T TRUST INVESTMENTS THAT DON'T COME THROUGH TRADITIONAL CHANNELS.

If you get a call or email or text from someone you've never heard of, never met, don't know anything about, who offers you a "great deal," please just hang up the phone or delete the email. Chances are, it's a scam. Now, if a broker from a reputable firm you have worked with for many years calls to offer you a great deal, keep listening.

If the information sounds interesting, at least do your research before investing in it, and then be cautious. Google the investment. Check with organizations such as FINRA and the SEC to make sure there are no complaints against the people sponsoring the investment. Ask the caller if you can talk to other investors, then verify, they're legitimate investors and not just office mates in the scam. The more questions you ask, the better the chance you will find a legitimate investment.

WHAT MAKES YOU SO SPECIAL?

We all pride ourselves on being smart, savvy investors. Whether you are or not, it's a good idea to set aside your pride long enough to wonder, "Why me?" If someone offers you an investment that sounds too good to be true, ask yourself why, among thousands of investors who might be interested, did this person or company offer you the chance to invest? Chances are it's not your investing savvy, as they will tell you. It's really their belief that based on your past investments, or other characteristics they thought you would be easy to scam. If you can't honestly come up with a good reason why you would be targeted for a "great investment opportunity," it's a very good idea to simply walk away.

THERE IS NO MAGIC BULLET — NO GET RICH QUICK OPPORTUNITY

Be cautious about offers of high returns with low risk. If the investment sounds too good to be true, chances are it is. And even if it is a legitimate, undiscovered gem, why would someone offer it to you, a stranger, and not their friends? Don't be so naive. You're more likely to be a mark or victim than someone a stranger wants to "help". Check out every investment carefully.

THERE'S NO RUSH. TAKE YOUR TIME.

The number one-way scammers, fraudsters, and schemers get people to invest in scams is by pressuring them into believing they don't have time to think, that they MUST act now or lose the opportunity. That's bogus. Don't be pressured into investing in anything immediately. If someone wants you to invest quickly, without taking time to do some research, there are some details they don't want you to know about. Take as much time as you need to research a potential investment before you decide to invest. If it's legit it will still be there in a week, or two, or even a month.

Finally, AARP warns these are signs you may be the target of a scammer:

- You receive a call from someone, or some company who pressures you to send money right away to take advantage of a supposedly once-in-a-lifetime opportunity.
- Someone or some company calls you and uses phrases such as "incredible gains," "breakout stock pick" or "huge upside and almost no risk!" The U.S. Securities and Exchange Commission (SEC) says such claims suggest high risk and possible fraud.
- Someone calls you with recommendations of foreign or "offshore" investments. If these come from someone you don't already know and trust, beware. Once your money is in another country, the SEC cautions, it's more difficult to keep watch over it.[81]

THINGS YOU SHOULDN'T DO WHEN INVESTING

- Never make investment decisions based upon TV commercials, phone calls or email solicitations. Today's marketing professionals are geniuses at making fraudulent investments sound and

---

[81] https://www.aarp.org/money/scams-fraud/info-2019/investment.html?

look legitimate. Don't be fooled by an investment opportunity that is offered by a company's attractive, professional-looking website. These days, crooks can easily create a convincing online facade.

- Don't get greedy. Con artists know that greed is the weakest link in a person. They know that dangling the prospect of fast and fabulous wealth will distract you from realizing their whole pitch is a scam.

- Just because you're in a chat room don't believe for a minute that everyone else there is just John or Jane Consumer/Investor just like you. Don't jump on the bandwagon of "inside" information posted to social media, chat rooms or forums promoting shares of a company that are 'certain to go up.' It could be a "pump-and-dump," which is a ploy to artificially drive up the price, allowing scammers to sell their shares for a big profit before the stock crashes and the remaining investors take a loss.

- Don't believe someone claiming to represent FINRA or the SEC-Securities Exchange Commission who offers an investment guarantee—these organizations along with its officers and employees do not do this. Some particularly audacious scammers pose as FINRA executives to create a false sense of security about an investment and secure an advance fee.

THINGS TO DO TO PROTECT YOUR INVESTMENT

I'm beating the drum again here. Educate yourself along with the help of your financial team thoroughly before you invest any money in anything. Once you find something you're interested in investing in, start asking questions—lots of questions. Do your homework. Considering investing in a publicly traded company? Before you take action, research information about its finances and operations in the SEC's EDGAR database. Some questions you should start out asking:

- What are the fees? What exactly do the fees cover?

- Have they registered the financial product with the SEC or state securities agencies?
- How does the investment company make money?
- What factors could affect the value of the investment?
- Who is handling the investment? (Do a background search in Broker Check, an online database maintained by the Financial Industry Regulatory Authority (FINRA), a nongovernmental group that watches over securities firms and dealers.)
- Be wary of free investment seminars, especially if they include a free lunch. The SEC reports that scammers often figure that by doing you a small favor, you'll feel obligated to invest.
- Have an exit strategy. FINRA advises that you rehearse some stock lines to cut short a caller's high-pressure pitch, such as, "I'm sorry, I'm not interested. Thank you."
- Do your homework. Prior to buying, only 20% of investors ever do a background check on brokers or products. Good starting points include the SEC's investor.gov (800-732-0330) and the Financial Industry Regulatory Authority's brokercheck.finra.org (800-289-9999).
- Look at the investor or firm. Research the SEC's EDGAR database for free corporate information, the fee-based pacer.gov to search federal lawsuits and bankruptcies, or your local courthouse for scams by area predators.
- Run from language like "risk-free," "guaranteed returns" and "everyone is doing it." Those terms should scare you off, not lull you into a feeling of safety.
- Churches, country clubs, community organizations and other safe spaces are happy hunting grounds for those pitching Ponzi schemes. Rely on your own research over referrals from friends, relatives, and celebrities. Celebrity endorsements don't mean an investment is legitimate. Celebrities can be fooled just as easily as you are.

- Don't be fooled by credentials. Those letters after the names of brokers and investment counselors can be meaningless. Many are outright fakes. Others are gained by paying a fee or taking a short online class. If a company or person is pushing their credentials take extra time to track down the issuing company and the legitimacy or proof of the credential.
- Have questions or need to file a complaint? Contact the SEC at 800-732-0330. Or get in touch with either FINRA at 844-57-HELPS, or the North American Securities Administrators Association at 202-737-0900. If you've been scammed, be sure to notify your local police, district attorney and state attorney general.

You work a lifetime to earn and save your money. Don't let it go easily and be extra careful when investing it.

CHAPTER TEN
AN INSPIRATIONAL STORY AND
TIPS TO GET YOU MOVING

Nothing gets me inspired, motivated and eager to try or do something new more than hearing, telling, or sharing an inspirational story. Hearing about how other people overcame a challenge or found a solution to an "impossible" problem reminds me that anything is possible. You'll probably find that as you get started with your spending plan, or the exercises I suggest you utilize to evaluate your financial worth and investment strategy that you may feel overwhelmed, discouraged, or hopeless. You're not alone. Until you get your money, retirement, and financial management skills under control it's common to feel those things. But you can and will get through those if you persist and hang in there. Others have, and you can too.

One of the most inspirational stories I tell my clients is about Taylor Swift, the country music singer. You likely know her name. I've known of her and her family since she was an undiscovered teenager growing up in Wyomissing, PA. This is the area where my practice originated. I know one of her neighbors whose husband used to dress up as Santa Claus and deliver Christmas presents to her family's home. That's why this story, along with all the Money Masters stories, is especially inspiring to me.

I remember back when Taylor Swift was in her teens, she sang at a local Chamber of Commerce event in Wyomissing, Pa. It was there that she sang the national anthem to start the evening. It was also at that event that she gave everyone a CD with a few of her personal recordings. At that point, she was still very young and going to the local high school. Her father was an advisor at Merrill Lynch and was already quite successful. One of her father's good friends was a local professional who I've known for over 30 years. Taylor's father asked this person if moving their family down to Tennessee to be closer to the country music capital would be advisable. This professional told me that he gave the following advice to Taylor's father: "I told her father it would be potentially financial suicide, since the odds of her reaching that level of success in Nashville were very slim." By the way, I am still very good friends with this business advisor. Knowing the slim odds for success this advice was likely very prudent at the time.

But her father, Scott Kingsley Swift, was no stranger to challenging odds, risks, and investments. After all, he was a seasoned investment advisor for Merrill Lynch and her mother, Andrea Gardner Swift (née Finlay), was a homemaker who had worked as a mutual fund marketing executive. They both understood that sometimes you have to take risks—financial or otherwise. They both supported and believed in their daughter. So, the decision was more than just financial. It was personal.

Taylor wasn't just another teenager dreaming of being a star either. After watching a documentary about Faith Hill and her climb to fame, Swift felt, as any aspiring singer would have, that she needed to go to Nashville, Tennessee, to pursue a music career.

At age eleven Taylor and her mom actually went to visit Nashville record labels and even submitted a demo tape of Dolly Parton and Dixie Chicks karaoke she had recorded to producers. Cue the rejections.

"Everyone in that town wanted to do what I wanted to do," she told writer Jim Malec after she became famous. "So, I kept thinking to myself, I need to figure out a way to be different." Inspired, not discouraged by the less than enthusiastic response to her demo tape, Taylor went back to the farm where she was raised and started learning how to play the guitar and how to write songs. She quickly discovered song writing, like singing, came naturally to her. When she returned to Nashville a little over a year later, she was a year older, wiser and much better prepared. She went armed with her own material, including *The Outside*, a song that made it onto her first album.

Had her father and family followed one of their friend's advice, she might not have gone to Nashville. "Too risky," people said. Had she not moved past the rejections, and looked for ways to stand out, she might not be the Pop Music star and multi-millionaire she is today.

You know the rest of the story. Shortly after her move to Nashville, Taylor became the youngest artist signed by the Sony/ATV Music publishing house. Now, having sold more than 50 million albums, including 32 million in the U.S., and 150 million singles, Taylor Swift is one of the best-selling music artists of all time. The odds against anyone having the same success as Taylor and her idol, Faith Hill, are huge, but not impossible. Taylor shared, "It didn't happen like it does in the movies. I look back and it seems like hundreds of thousands of tiny baby steps that lead to that moment."

So why am I so inspired, and what can Taylor Swift's story teach you? I think the number one takeaway for me is "believe in yourself and your dreams even when those around you are telling you not to." But there's more:

1. **You've got to make sure that your professional team is on the same page as you are.** Most of us don't have the time, energy, or resources to argue or prove ourselves to naysayers. It's fine to listen, but don't take it to heart. Even though you might not always get prodded in a direction you think you want to go, you have to weigh the good and the bad, then go with your instincts. At the end of the day, you have to be true to your goals and your dreams. Don't let anybody steal it away from you with

a negative connotation. Let them give you some positive ways to minimize that risk, and like Taylor did, look for ways to make it happen. It's rare that anyone in any field succeeds the first time they try. We build success from the ashes of our failures.

2. **Ignore the naysayers.** How many times have you been told in life that you can't achieve this or that? That you're never going to arrive "there," wherever "there" is for you? Logic would tell you (or your family members) that you can't accomplish your dreams. Taylor's parents took a contrarian view to logic, though, and thankfully so! What I suggest is to take more of a blended approach that balances your dreams, which are very important to achieve various life goals, with calculated risks.

3. **Don't give up.** Find an alternative approach. Not everyone gets in through the same door. Taylor realized that every young girl in Nashville had the same dream she did. She needed to find a way to be different, to stand out, to get people's attention. She took a year to learn how to play guitar and become a songwriter. It might not have worked for other young singers, but she made it work for her. Just because someone tells you it "can't work, won't work, or is a crazy idea" doesn't mean they're correct. What gives them the right to tell anyone what can or can't work? Most of the inventions on the market today were products of a mistake. People rarely make what they set out to invent. They often find something bigger, better, and more profitable. Never give up. You may be on the verge of something big.

4. **Set achievable goals.** Eliminating debt can feel overwhelming, especially if the amount you owe is more than you make in a couple of years. It doesn't matter if you owe $50,000 and make $30,000 and can barely get by, or if you owe $100,000 and make $75,000 a year. You can set a goal of $1,000, or $5,000 or

$10,000 and work towards that. Once you've reached that, set another goal.

Dave Ramsey encourages his followers to save $1,000 for their emergency fund. Some people can knock that off in a couple of months, for others it takes a year. The point is, make it an achievable goal for you.

Focus on your endgame, not on the challenges. Taylor Swift focused on how she could be different, what she needed to do and learn to advance towards her goal. Her demo tape was initially rejected but she didn't sit around licking her wounds and crying. She focused on what she needed to do to stand out, and on her end goal — being a musician. Maybe your goal is to finish college, to start a business, to retire and travel, or just to retire comfortably. Whatever it is, write it down and read it every day. It sounds simple, but it's profoundly powerful.

If you want more inspiring stories like Taylor Swift's I encourage you to read the books and websites I list at the end of this book. While Taylor Swift and many of our Financial Masters have inspiring stories, there are thousands of stories from Dave Ramsey's site about ordinary people who got serious, followed his 'financial snowball' plan and paid off thousands, or even hundreds of thousands of dollars in debt in only a few years. It can be done. Just ask Dave Ramsey follower Ty'Lisha and her husband.

According to Dave Ramsey's website the couple racked up more than $100,000 in student loan and other debt once they graduated from college. They followed Dave Ramsey's "snowball approach" (List your debts from smallest to largest, regardless of interest rate. Step 2: With the exception of your smallest debt, make minimum payments on all other debts. Step 3: Pay the maximum you can afford on your smallest debt. Step 4: Repeat the process until each debt is fully paid off. When the smallest debt is paid in full, you roll the money you were paying on that debt into the next smallest balance.) It took them eight years, but they paid it off.

While it's easy to say, "It only took eight years"—think about that for a moment. Eight years is 96 months, or 416 weeks. That's a lot of denying yourself immediate gratification!

What I've often found that is missing in many of these stories is how hard, challenging, or frightening it is to look at your debt. One must form a workable plan to eliminate debt, while finding the discipline and courage to stick with it. You may initially fail, but what matters most is that you get back up and get back on track. The tips that worked for Taylor Swift will work for you too. Finally, one more thing to think about:

FINANCIAL EDGE QUESTION:

From whom are you currently taking the majority of your financial advice? As you can probably tell from many of my stories, my clients rely on family, friends, CPA's, bankers, and a variety of financial advisors (myself included) when making decisions. They also look to books, podcasts, and financial media to glean the majority of their financial advice.

While I'm all for collecting and sifting through advice from a variety of sources, I strongly urge you to find a good financial advisor and/or a team that can help you with your financial decisions over time. Don't just depend on that advisor. Educate yourself and meet with them regularly. Learn, question and take an active role in managing your money. When you find a good, trustworthy financial advisor they should be committed to the "Fiduciary Standard" by "Always putting your best interests first." To find an independent Fiduciary Advisor go to the site: www.findyourindependenantadvisor.com.

CHAPTER ELEVEN
SUMMARY

In an acceptance speech I watched some time ago, actor Tom Hanks had a bit of advice that not many of us would consider financial advice. He said, "The best thing you can do is to bet on yourself to win."

No one else knows what you can do, and you won't know unless you try. The way to live and to not look back with regrets is to simply go for it. Bet on yourself.

I remembered this when I had to fire my CPA. I was looking to launch my mutual fund and was telling him about it. He literally said, "Who is going to invest with you to launch a fund like this?" He was pretty condescending to me as I was sitting there with my lawyer. So, I fired him.

The next day I sent off a letter to him stating, "I haven't gotten to where I am by having people weigh me down with negative input. I was looking for positive input. Yes, you obviously had some concerns, but your concerns are not in line with my goals and objectives." Then I went and found another CPA.

If I were to have listened to him, I never would have launched the very successful mutual fund that we managed at the time. It was one of the Penn Street Funds called, The Berkshire Select Equity Portfolio made up of only large cap dividend paying companies. The fund was named, Berkshire Select Equity Portfolio after my deep admiration of Warren

Buffett's stock management discipline and my RIA company, Berkshire Advisors, Inc.

I also would never have been recognized by the Wall Street Journal's *"Category Kings" segment,* over a dozen times for its historical above average returns, along with recognition by Barron's, USA Today and Morningstar.

And yes, I had a great quantitative money management team, legal team and shareholder accounting company team. Ultimately, I would have lost out on one of my lifetime dreams had I listened to a particular professional that I was fairly confident with up until that time.

I'm not alone in recognizing team members who need to be fired. Lori Greiner, of *Shark Tank* and QVC fame knew rudeness and non-supportiveness when she experienced it personally. According to Influencive.com "Greiner had just paid $5,000 to file her first patent for an earring organizer. The money had come from savings she shared with her husband Dan, so he accompanied her in a meeting with the patent attorney. Dan sat off to the side, since it was Lori's invention and he was just there as an observer, or so he and Lori thought.

After ten minutes of watching the attorney speak mostly to her husband, and not to her, she told him she was 'done with the rude way he was treating her,' and asked for one of the firm's partners and then asked him to send in a female attorney. Natalie Kadievitch became the female attorney who replaced him, and she has worked with Greiner ever since. Imagine the money the original attorney threw away all because he failed to grasp the simple fact it was her business, not her husband's and to treat her with respect. Such a simple thing, yet I guarantee you so many people don't get it. It's up to you to stop them and kick them off the team the minute you become aware they're not a good fit for you.

In her book *Invent it, Sell it, Bank it*, Greiner writes that it's important to call out injustices, "but be polite even as you do it."[82]

Sometimes it's necessary to fire even those we once considered successors to our operations. Warren Buffett has certainly not let former relationships interfere with his firing employees. David L. Sokol was once one of Buffett's top lieutenants. He was even considered a potential successor to Buffett.

In March of 2011, he abruptly resigned after it came to light that he had bought about $10 million in shares of stock in Lubrizol Corp. before suggesting that Berkshire buy the chemical company (which it did).

At first Buffett said he didn't feel Sokols trades were "in any way unlawful." however, weeks later he called it "inexcusable" and said the trades violated Berkshire's code of ethics. Berkshire's audit committee delivered a scathing 18-page report. (Nonetheless, Sokol's departure didn't warrant a mention in Buffett's annual letter to shareholders for that year.)[83] Buffett is reluctant, for whatever reason, to mention people he's fired, but Jordan Hansell, Richard Santulli, Denis Abrams, and Robert Merritt, all fell under Buffett's axe for various reasons—most having to do with transgressing one or more of Buffett's promises and ethics to his companies and stockholders.

Don't be afraid to make changes to your staff or support group if need be. People change, we change. Do what's best for you regardless of what your "experts" are saying, even if they insist. Trust your gut. You may be wrong and may lose, but you may be right. Either way, you won't kick yourself for listening to someone else.

---

[82] https://www.eonline.com/news/912184/how-shark-tank-s-lori-greiner-earned-her-queen-of-qvc-title

[83] https://www.marketwatch.com/story/5-times-warren-buffett-has-said-youre-fired-2016-02-27

No matter what, you're still the one to make the decision. No matter what, if you fall on hard times, you can recover. If you have one to ten people in your life that you admire who are living a life that you want to emulate, you're only as strong as your weakest link. If you have those people in your life, chances are you're going to find yourself living up instead of dumbing yourself down. You are the sum total of the 5-10 people you spend the most time with — whether those people are co-workers, or family or part of both.

I have numerous types of personal and professional friends and we're all a bit different. I think of one of them, whose nickname is Mr. P. He tends to be quite negative at times. He admits that he is negative although he owns a highly profitable business and has been an avid athlete his whole life. Among our friends he has earned the nickname Mr. P. for Mr. Pessimistic. He's a good golfing friend of mine and several of us travel frequently together with our wives. However, his stamina, endurance, competitive and positive energy relating to his athletic endeavors is truly amazing.

I say to my wife, "We are truly blessed to have a variety of friends." I believe we all gather or gain some sort of momentum from each other. They gain a positive attitude and energy that helps them in their life, even though they're producing similar energy for you. People are naturally attracted to *different* people. Some days we have the energy to share. Some days we don't. When we have that energy to share, I think people gravitate towards that because they know we're genuine people.

When you have friends that are top performers, partnering with them in some way benefits everyone involved. Most people don't think about that. You must always make sure you're surrounding yourself with people that will encourage you to follow your dream versus telling you that you can't do it. Friends become a pretty important part of your success moving ahead. Daymond John tweets and speaks about the importance of surrounding yourself with positive people.

"Surround yourself with like-minded people who focus on success and positivity. They'll pick you up when you need it most," he said.[84]

I know. It's impossible to have 100% positive friends, or to be 100% positive ourselves always, but we can set that as a goal. I love how Tony Robbins addresses negativity in ourselves. He advocates a cold-water plunge, or shower to start the day, an "attitude of gratitude," prayer or meditation, and breathing exercises. It may sound silly, but the fact is, his process is scientifically proven to boost our mood.

Our vagus nerve, for instance, is an important part of our parasympathetic nervous system. This nerve connects many organs, such as the brain, heart, liver, and gut. When we stimulate it with cold water, or cold air, we can increase the "vagal tone," which has a positive effect on our mood. Having a "low vagal tone" means that the vagus nerve is impaired, usually due to stress. A low vagal tone results in things like anxiety, depression, gut problems, and inflammation. We can't stimulate the nerve directly, but we can affect it by treating the organs it's connected to.

Deep breathing: Deep breathing activates specific neurons that detect blood pressure. These neurons signal to the vagus nerve that blood pressure is becoming too high, and the vagus nerve in turn responds by lowering your heart rate.[85]

Expressing Gratitude: Robbins says that "you cannot be grateful and angry, or grateful and fearful at the same time." Gratitude can detoxify your mind of negativity. Robbins isn't the only expert to talk about gratitude, which is why I keep coming back to it. It's powerful.

Gratitude can be expressed anywhere, anytime. No special equipment needed. Some people find it helpful to write down, or keep a journal of what they're grateful for, but all you really need to do is sit and count

---

[84] https://twitter.com/TheSharkDaymond/status/839273695050878977
[85] https://www.wimhofmethod.com/vagus-nerve-stimulation

off in your head a few things you feel thankful for. These things could include your car running well, lunch with a friend you haven't seen in a while, a parking spot right out front when you were running late. It can be having a new creative idea for work, a job you love, money to pay for an unexpected bill. Leaders and experts from Oprah to the Harvard Business Review have talked about the difference gratitude can make in our lives. Gratitude can help us gain a new perspective of what is important to us and what we truly appreciate in our lives.

If you journal your daily gratitude you become more aware of what matters to you and help gain clarity on what you want more of in your life, and what you want less of as well. Gratitude helps us focus on what is happening in our lives and helps us become more aware of who we are.

Meditation or Prayer: Meditation isn't just sitting around chanting. Mindfulness is the basic human ability to be fully present in each moment. It means being aware of where we are and what we're doing, thinking and feeling, and not being overly reactive or overwhelmed by what's going on around us. Mindful meditation is a discipline, an act of sitting still and paying attention to our thoughts, and our feelings. Feelings arise out of our thoughts. It may seem the other way around, but once you notice your thoughts, you'll be able to see they are what spark our emotions. When you learn to recognize and change your thoughts, you'll be able to change your emotions as well. It's science.[86]

Singing: Singing, humming, and gargling activate your vocal cords and the muscles in the back of your throat, which are connected to the vagus nerve. Incorporating these activities into your daily routine can help increase your vagal tone.[87]

Acute Cold: Taking a cold shower or splashing cold water on your face, increases stimulation of the vagus nerve. While your body adjusts to the cold, sympathetic activity (the fight or flight response, like hitting the

---

[86] https://www.mindful.org/mindfulness-how-to-do-it/
[87] https://www.wimhofmethod.com/vagus-nerve-stimulation

gas in our car, this system speeds up our responses) declines, while parasympathetic activity (like hitting the brakes, our parasympathetic system calms us and slows down our responses) increases.

EDUCATE YOURSELF ABOUT MONEY

"Sometimes parents wait until their kids are in their teens before they start talking about managing money—when they could be starting when their kids are in preschool," Warren Buffet says.

Other money experts agree, saying that financial education for kids can and should start around 3 years old. That's when "executive function," or the brain's mental muscle, begins to develop. "There's not a huge difference in absorbing financial information and other information," says Elizabeth Odders-White, associate dean at the University of Wisconsin-Madison's Wisconsin School of Business. "By age 3, children begin to develop cognitive control; their brains are ready and able to learn," she said in a 2015 interview with creditcard.com.[88]

If you're an adult who didn't learn about money until college, or even later in life, it's never too late to learn. The thing is, as an adult learner studies show, you'll learn best if you feel out of your comfort zone, and you fail. Those are the two things most of us hate, but they're also the things that ensure we actually do learn and retain new information. So when you're feeling panicked and scared, or you blow your spending plan the first few times around, remind yourself you're learning!

Daymond John readily admits his lack of financial knowledge hurt him in the beginning. He urges others to educate themselves about money, business, and life. "If you don't educate yourself, you'll never get out of the starting block because you'll spend all your money-making foolish decisions."[89]

---

[88] https://www.creditcards.com/credit-card-news/kids-know-money-age-1279.php
[89] https://addicted2success.com/quotes/35-motivating-daymond-john-quotes/

If you're intimidated by learning through websites or books with adult financial materials, it's okay to find some apps or websites for kids and teens and learn there. They can be much easier to understand, more user friendly, and have the same information as adult financial sites.

Wherever or however you learn, there are four things you must teach yourself and your children about money:

- **Work.** You must earn your money. Our society is moving more and more into an "entitled" mindset, but don't be misled. Work, whether you work for yourself, or at a job, or through investing, or creating passive income, is where money comes from — it doesn't grow on trees and it's not free, and it's not the responsibility of others to ensure we have it.

- **Give.** Most kids give naturally from generous hearts, adults, not so much. Dave Ramsey, who is a Christian, recommends giving 10% of your income (he calls it tithing) even when you're paying off your debt and while getting your spending in order.[90] Other experts, Christian or not, also recommend setting aside 10% of your income to give. Giving, they say, is part of being a responsible member of society. Whatever your reasons for giving or tithing, set aside some part of your income to help others. Call it karma, or God's reward, or life, it does return to you when you need it most.

- **Save.** The amount you save out of each paycheck will vary according to your personal goals, but the rule of thumb for savings is 10-15% for retirement, and whatever you need to accumulate six months of your monthly expenses for an emergency. If you need $1,200 or $12,000 a month to meet your rent/mortgage, utilities, insurance, cell phone payments, food, and whatever then figure out what you need to save from each check to reach that number.

---

[90] https://www.daveramsey.com/blog/give-while-in-debt

- **Spend wisely.** Spending is the fun part, right? Only if you have a spending plan so the money you must spend goes towards the items in your budget. Spend in a way that enhances your life. Invest, give, save and enjoy the fruits of your labor.

Once you have the basics and the discipline down and your debt paid off or being paid off, start learning about investing, real estate, and how to make your money grow. This is where a team of financial advisors, or just a financial advisor to begin with, comes in. Take some classes. Read. Listen to podcasts. Pursue education in ways and at levels that make sense to you. Try one or more of the Apps listed under Resources at the end of this book. Sometimes an app can make learning, saving, and investing make more sense, especially if you've grown up in a digital culture.

CHANGE YOUR MONEY MENTALITY

I can't tell you how many people have come to me or cornered me at parties to talk about money who supposedly understand money. They just don't understand how the wrong money mentality can derail them. It may well sound like some type of magic, with no foundation in science or fact, but it is science-based. The psychology of money is real and how we think and feel about our money, and about whether we deserve it or not will impact how well we earn and manage our money. If you're uncomfortable with money and your feelings about it, find a way to address those feelings, either with an advisor, a therapist, spouse, or someone you trust. Work on changing your feelings about money and watch your entire relationship with it change as well.

BELIEVE IN YOURSELF AND YOUR DREAMS

I've told numerous stories about firing or not listening to naysayers who try to crush your dreams throughout this book. I talk about the importance of believing in yourself and your dreams for a reason. It's because no one else is going to step up and encourage, support or push you to chase your dreams if you're not doing that already. It's up to you to decide what you want out of life and to pursue it. Those dreams can be personal, like Taylor Swift's Nashville dream to sing; or they can be financial—wanting security and a home, and financial independence. What matters is they're your dreams, not your spouse's, or parents, or friends, or society or the people you know on Facebook. If they're not your dreams and goals when things get tough, you're not going to persist.

I hope you've found insight and inspiration and answers to some of your questions about money and money management in these chapters and stories. I hope you keep learning, researching, and exploring the world of money and finance. If you don't have a budget or spending plan, I really hope you are now motivated to start creating one today. Don't wait. Remember, money is a tool, and one we all need to be able to use wisely. If this book doesn't speak to you right now, give it a few weeks or months and read it again. Explore some of the additional resources, books, podcasts and articles listed in the resource section. Whatever you do, learn to understand your relationship with money and act to ensure you have enough to make your life what you want it to be.

ACKNOWLEDGEMENTS

I want to thank my family for all their ongoing support they have given me over the years for all my business endeavors. To my soulmate and wife Jennifer, for her love, encouragement and commitment to me in every aspect of my career. Also, for her belief in me to finalize my ideas and writings in order to publish this book.

For my mom and dad who have given me a moral and ethical compass to follow and taught me the importance of diligence and honest hard work. Special remembrance to my dad for all the daily lifetime "Talks" and his "Never a Doubt" attitude of where my financial journey would take me in life.

To Melissa G Wilson and my publishing team at Networlding Publishing. Thank you for all the consulting, mentoring, education and guidance over the last 5 years. I could not have gotten to the finish line without your consistent endorsement, book writing and publishing experience.

For all the "Financial Experts" highlighted in this book and their real-life advice to all those who are willing to learn & listen. To Warren Buffet, David Bach, Ronald S. Baron, Harry Dent, Lori Greiner, Damon John, The Napoleon Hill Foundation, Robert Kiyosaki, Mike Michalowicz, Suzie Orman, Dave Ramsey and Tony Robbins. Thank you for inspiring this book and for sharing your life's experiences to all of us through your life's work and dedication to "Making a Difference."

RESOURCES

APPS

There are a lot of ways to track your spending — either on paper with pen, online, or through a variety of free or for a monthly fee apps. Here are some of the most popular in alphabetical order:

Acorns

Acorns is a painless way for users, especially college students, to save. Acorns rounds up your purchases on the credit and debit cards you link to the app. The difference is automatically transferred to an Acorns account. This account is part of Acorns investing platform. Your money savings are then invested in exchange-traded funds. You get the option to invest in conservative or aggressive funds based on what you feel comfortable doing. College students get to use Acorns for free for up to four years. Everyone else has to pay a monthly fee if your account is under $5,000 or a percentage fee on anything above that amount in your account. https://www.acorns.com/

Clarity Money — Free App

Clarity Money clarifies wise spending from wasteful spending by cancelling subscriptions you are not using or just don't need. It also looks for ways to negotiate your bills down to a lower rate. You'll earn as you learn because Clarity recommends certain credit cards that fit your lifestyle and credit needs, although be careful when using credit cards. This app works by tracking what you've spent to ensure you stay on budget.

You can create a savings account with Clarity Money to put all the money you're saving.
https://apps.apple.com/US/app/id1148133022?mt=8

HoneyFi

HoneyFi is a free money-saving app that helps couples work together to make the most of their money. It's no secret that couples argue about money, how to earn it, save it, and spend it. This app helps take the animosity out of finances by simplifying, organizing and tracking a couple/family's finances by eliminating mistrust around spending. For example, you can create a household budget, label and comment on transactions, and share information on all accounts and statements.
https://www.honeyfi.com/

Mint

Mint was rated the number one financial app by Investopedia for 2019. Hands down, the free Mint app from Intuit Inc. (INTU)—the company behind QuickBooks and TurboTax—is an effective all-in-one resource for creating a budget, tracking your spending, and getting smart about your money. Although Mint doesn't work with all banks or credit unions, it works with a majority of them. Check to see if your bank works with Mint before signing up. Mint helps you stay on top of your bills, so you aren't late don't end up costing yourself more money than you need to spend on late fees and penalties. Mint helps you develop a budget to ensure you maximize what you can do with your money and allocate money for savings, an emergency fund, and retirement while covering all your other obligations. You'll also be able to get a free credit score to monitor how your savings. Mint is currently only available in the U.S. and Canada. The app, Emma, is the U.K. alternative.
https://mint.com

Robinhood

Want to learn more about investing? Try Robinhood, a game-changing investing app with a very unique and unbeatable feature: Transactions are free for stocks, ETFs (some 2,000 of them), options, and American depositary receipts (ADRs). The app makes money by upselling premium services like margin trading and payment for order flow. It's also one of the very first personal investing apps to offer Bitcoin trading capabilities. Along with no commissions, there are no account minimums or maintenance fees.

Special features: "Cards" appear on your screen to give you real-time news alerts and market information. They sound intrusive, but they're actually helpful, and you can customize them or opt-out altogether. If you're brand new to investing, this can bring you up-to-speed pretty quickly. https://robinhood.com/

Find Your Independent Advisor & Smart Assets

Both sites offer free financial tools and can direct you to fiduciary based financial advisors in your area in minutes. These advisors are legally bound to "ALWAYS" act in your best interests. If you're ready to be matched with local advisors that will help you achieve your financial goals, get started now. https://findyourindependentadvisor.net;

https://Smartasset.com

Trim

Think of Trim like your very own personal financial assistant. By linking all your accounts within the app, it can analyze each transaction and suggest areas to cut back on or eliminate, like game subscriptions or all those trips to the coffee shop.

Once all your accounts (anything you spend money on) are linked, Trim finds more affordable service providers for things like cable, car insurance, and the internet. It will even cancel subscriptions for you. You'll be able to get text updates on how your accounts are doing and immediately see any automated changes that have been made. This is a great option for most self-employed people looking for a personalized financial assistant.

Tycoon

Tycoon is Investopedia's top pick for apps for freelancers. It was founded by a freelancer (supermodel Jess Perez, whose portfolio includes posing for Victoria's Secret and Sports Illustrated' s swimsuit edition) for freelancers. Freelancers are often paid very late for their work, sometimes months or even years after the contractually required payment period. Not only that, keeping up with multiple projects can be hard, especially since they're usually in the middle of another project when a new one comes in.

Though popular with those in the fashion industry (photographers, stylists, etc.), Tycoon can be valuable for any self-employed person. It lets you standardize the details of a gig, put in a timetable for it, and keep track of payments that have come in, are scheduled to come in, or that are past due—your own little balance sheet, so to speak. It also makes it easy to see, at a glance, which clients have not paid you yet. Because Tycoon caters to a freelancer's special needs, such as calculating take-home pay (minus taxes and agent commission) you can decide whether or not to even accept a new gig.

YNAB (You Need A Budget)

You Need a Budget (YNAB) is an app that helps you create an easy-to-use budget interface that teaches you more about the value of money. YNAB helps you stop living paycheck to paycheck, pay down debt, and "roll with the punches" if something unexpected comes up. It's built around a fairly simple principle: Every dollar has a "job" in your personal budget, be it for investing, for debt repayment, or to cover living expenses. Learn to prioritize certain expenses, find ways to save more money for retirement and emergencies, handle unexpected costs, and live within your means, rather than using credit. The company offers the app and software that works on your Windows or Mac computer. It works for all mobile devices for iOS and Android as well as Apple Watch and Amazon's Alexa.

GAMES ABOUT MONEY

Let's face it, kids rarely see real money anymore. They see us swipe our credit or debit cards or wave our smart phones at a payment terminal. The days of coins and cash are fast disappearing. What they do know are games. So, what better way to teach them (or you!) about money than fun games like:

- Monopoly
- Junior monopoly
- Life
- Buy it Right
- Pay Day

There are dozens of video and online games as well. Explore and find games that best fit you and your family.

- Money Metropolis
- Financial Football
- Cash Puzzler
- Road Trip to Savings
- Financial Soccer
- Countdown to Retirement

There are also hundreds of Free online banking and money management courses and classes. Your bank may offer their own courses, or you can start here:

https://study.com/articles/List_of_Free_Online_Banking_Courses_Training_and_Tutorials.html

http://www.freeonlinecoursesforall.com/2014/09/26/10-free-online-courses-to-learn-basics-of-banking/

ARTICLES

Best Millennial Money Blogs
https://millennialmoney.com/best-millennial-money-blogs/

15 Investing Failures Warren Buffet Regrets
https://www.cnbc.com/2017/12/15/warren-buffetts-failures-15-investing-mistakes-he-regrets.html

Teaching Kids About Money, An Age by Age Guide
https://www.parents.com/parenting/money/family-finances/teaching-kids-about-money-an-age-by-age-guide/

Reasons Not to Own a Home
https://www.thesimpledollar.com/loans/home/does-it-make-sense-to-never-own-a-home/

WEBSITES

Get Rich Education (Keith Weinhold)

https://www.getricheducation.com/

Books:

7 Money Myths That Are Killing Your Wealth Potential - a reality check on conventional thinking, with practical solutions you can implement to create lasting wealth.

The Passive Income Guide: What is Your Return on Life? - a how-to manual for leveraging investment options in real estate to create passive income

Podcasts:

https://www.getricheducation.com/podcast/

THE MASTERS BOOKS, LINKS, and MORE

David Bach

You can learn more about David Bach's books, seminars, and training by visiting www.davidbach.com.

Books:

Smart Women Finish Rich - a best seller for more than 20 years, with more than one million copies sold. A roadmap for women toward clear control and confidence.

The Latte Factor: Why You Don't Have to Be Rich to Live Rich - a compelling, demystifying parable that will assist you in modifying your path for lifetime impact.

The Automatic Millionaire: A Powerful One-Step Plan to Live and Finish Rich - a realistic system based upon solid foundational precepts to create financial security in your future.

Start Late, Finish Rich: A No-Fail Plan for Achieving Financial Freedom at Any Age - stop living paycheck to paycheck with an easy, inspiring plan complete with worksheets and full instructions.

The Finish Rich Workbook: Creating a Personalized Plan for a Richer Future (Get out of debt, Put your dreams in action and achieve Financial Freedom - organize your financial life and put together a quick plan with timed to-do lists and systems.

Smart Couples Finish Rich: 9 Steps to Creating a Rich Future for You and Your Partner - warm advice and solid techniques to manage and plan your future in alignment with your values and goals as a couple.

The Automatic Millionaire: A Powerful One-Step Plan to Live and Finish Rich - gain financial freedom from debt with easy, automatic and painless methods.

The Automatic Millionaire Workbook: A Personalized Plan to Live and Finish Rich. . . Automatically - written as a companion piece to The Automatic Millionaire, the workbook has charts, checklists, and worksheets to create your game plan.

The Automatic Millionaire Homeowner: A Powerful Plan to Finish Rich in Real Estate - an easy-to-follow plan to harness the financial benefits of home ownership to achieve lasting financial growth

Debt Free For Life: The Finish Rich Plan for Financial Freedom (with co-authors) - an innovative approach to financial freedom, using a ground-breaking, timed approach to debt elimination and early retirement.

Podcasts:

http://betteroffpodcast.com/better-off-podcast-ep1/

http://podcast.farnoosh.tv/episode/david-bach/

https://www.stitcher.com/podcast/the-latte-factor-podcast

https://lewishowes.com/podcast/be-financially-free-and-pay-yourself-first-with-david-bach/

https://podcasts.apple.com/us/podcast/98-how-anyone-can-be-financially-free-with-david-bach/id1245763628?i=1000439915443

https://consciousmillionaire.com/davidbach/

Ronald S. Baron

You can learn more about Ronald Baron's books, seminars, and training by visiting https://www.baronfunds.com/insights and https://www.baronfunds.com/baron-conference

Warren Buffett

You can learn more about Warren Buffett's books, seminars, and training by visiting www.berkshirehathaway.com

Books:

The Essays of Warren Buffett: Lessons for Corporate America - views on investing, corporate management, edited for a streamlined read.

Berkshire Hathaway Letters to Shareholders - Fifty years of unedited communications share methods and lessons in Buffett's own words. Includes topic index and growth charts.

Podcasts:

https://player.fm/podcasts/Warren-Buffett

Harry Dent

You can learn more about Harry Dent's books, seminars, and training by visiting www.harrydent.com

Books:

Zero Hour: Turn the Greatest Political and Financial Upheaval in Modern History to Your Advantage. Harry Dent reveals why the greatest social, economic, and political upheaval since the American Revolution is on our doorstep and arms you with the tools you need to financially prepare and survive in the coming financial crisis.

The Demographic Cliff: How to Survive and Prosper During the Great Deflation of 2014-2019.

Zero Hour: Turn the Greatest Political and Financial Upheaval in Modern History to Your Advantage.

The Sale of a Lifetime: How the Great Bubble Burst of 2017-2019 Can Make You Rich.

Spending Waves: The Scientific Key to Predicting Market Behavior for the Next 20 Years.

Lori Greiner

You can learn more about Lori Greiner's books, seminars, and training by visiting www.lorigreiner.com

Books:

Invent It, Sell It, Bank It! Make Your Million-Dollar Idea into a Reality - turn your vision into a product or a company with information and actionable advice

Podcasts:

Talking About Business https://podcasts.apple.com/us/podcast/shark-tank-lori-greiner/id1329265940?i=1000424236545

https://podtail.com/en/podcast/success-talks/lori-greiner-on-being-a-hero-not-a-zero/

http://disunplugged.com/tag/lori-greiner/

Daymond John

You can learn more about Daymond John's books, seminars, and training by visiting www.daymondjohn.com

Books:

Display of Power - a blueprint for young entrepreneurs to achieve success and growth as evidenced by the FUBU brand

The Brand Within: The Power of Branding from Birth to the Boardroom (2010) - an examination of branding tactics from celebrity endorsements to impulse purchasing influences.

The Power of Broke: How Empty Pockets, a Tight Budget, and a Hunger for Success Can Become Your Greatest Competitive Advantage - how "desperation breeds innovation" to your greater competitive advantage.

Rise & Grind: Outperform, Outwork, and Outhustle Your Way to a More Successful and Rewarding Life - how a determined work ethic, drive, and performance make the biggest difference in a personal success story you craft.

Powershift: Transform Any Situation, Close Any Deal, and Achieve Any Outcome - use your reputation, negotiating ability, and leverage in your relationships to close the important deals with lasting benefits.

Podcasts:

https://podcasts.apple.com/us/podcast/rise-and-grind-with-daymond-john/id1335405828

Napoleon Hill

You can learn more about Napoleon Hill's books, seminars, and training by visiting https://www.naphill.org

Books:

Think and Grow Rich: The Original, an Official Publication of The Napoleon Hill Foundation - the classic, original laws of success with basic techniques to achieve understanding and rewarding business and personal relationships.

Napoleon Hill's Success Principles Rediscovered (Official Publication of the Napoleon Hill Foundation) - timeless tips and wisdom ready to use in your personal circumstances.

Think and Grow Rich: The Landmark Bestseller Now Revised and Updated for the 21st Century (Think and Grow Rich Series) - updated with contemporary anecdotes with contemporary language edits.

Robert Kiyosaki

You can learn more about Robert Kiyosaki's books, seminars, and training by visiting https://www.richdad.com/

Books:

FAKE: Fake Money, Fake Teachers, Fake Assets: How Lies Are Making the Poor and Middle Class Poorer - learn to discern what's fact or fake about conventional wisdom, using insights and financial acumen.

Rich Dad's Cashflow Quadrant: Guide to Financial Freedom - how to exert control over your finances and your future by changing your thinking.

Rich Dad Poor Dad: What the Rich Teach Their Kids About Money That the Poor and Middle Class Do Not! - the 20th anniversary edition of the classic story with updates to reflect changes in the global economy and proof of the timelessness in the original.

The Business of the 21st Century - an examination of multi-level marketing with contextual insights into its relevance and universality.

Rich Dad's Guide to Investing: What the Rich Invest in, That the Poor and the Middle Class Do Not! - basic investing rules take you from a passive bystander to an active and engaged strategist.

Why the Rich Are Getting Richer - the gap is getting wider, but why? Learn how debt, taxes and savings interplay with conventional "wisdom" to keep people poor.

Rich Dad's Increase Your Financial IQ: Get Smarter with Your Money - work on your financial intelligence to identify new options and paths in a turbulent financial landscape.

Podcasts:

https://www.richdad.com/radio

Mike Michalowicz

You can learn more about Mike Michalowicz' s books, seminars, and training by visiting https://mikemichalowicz.com/

Books:

Fix This Next: Make the Vital Change That Will Level Up Your Business - ways to identify exactly what the problem is to prioritize the necessary modifications for growth.

Profit First: Transform Your Business from a Cash-Eating Monster to a Money-Making Machine - solve your cash management problems with a simple, yet elegantly counterintuitive transformation.

Clockwork: Design Your Business to Run Itself - strategic design to free you from the day to day by empowering employees and identifying functional priorities.

The Pumpkin Plan: A Simple Strategy to Grow a Remarkable Business in Any Field - innovative growth strategies to nurture your business into a flourishing success.

The Toilet Paper Entrepreneur: The Tell-it-Like-it-is Guide to Cleaning Up in Business, Even if You Are at the End of Your Roll - a "reality check approach" to take your business from launch to thrive.

Surge: Time the Marketplace, Ride the Wave of Consumer Demand, and Become Your Industry's Big Kahuna - a trend identification process to anticipate and respond to upcoming consumer behavior, wants and needs.

Podcasts:

https://mikemichalowicz.com/podcast/

Suze Orman

You can learn more about Suze Orman's books, seminars, and training by visiting www.suzeorman.com

Books:

Women & Money (Revised and Updated) - #1 New York Times best-seller, with over one million copies sold, enables you to take the financial reins using compassionate and practical advice.

The 9 Steps to Financial Freedom: Practical and Spiritual Steps So You Can Stop Worrying - a refreshed version of the classic edition which changed how we think about money more than fifteen years ago.

The Money Book for the Young, Fabulous & Broke - for members of "Generation Debt," a solution-based guide to the contemporary financial landscape.

The Road to Wealth - updated from the original 2001 edition, a financial reference blueprint containing practical and actionable advice, particularly for financial novices.

Suze Orman's Financial Guidebook: Put the 9 Steps to Work - transformational, motivational and inspirational practical guidance in a user-friendly workbook format.

The Money Class: Learn to Create Your New American Dream - a nine-section course which strategically empowers you as a caretaker, breadwinner, and investor.

Podcasts:

https://www.suzeorman.com/podcast

Dave Ramsey

You can learn more about Dave Ramsey's books, seminars, and training by visiting www.daveramsey.com

Books:

Dave Ramsey's Complete Guide To Money - Financial Peace University's handbook, a complete all-in-one resource guide from the most trusted source in America.

The Financial Peace Planner: A Step-by-Step Guide to Restoring Your Family's Financial Health - a workbook to assess, understand, and address the areas that are affecting your financial peace of mind.

Financial Peace Revisited: New Chapters on Marriage, Singles, Kids and Families - updated techniques and principles to guide sound financial decision-making.

The Total Money Makeover: A Proven Plan for Financial Fitness - a blunt, no-nonsense game plan for reorganizing, reassessing, and revising your money habits for asset retention and a secure future.

The Total Money Makeover Workbook: Classic Edition: The Essential Companion for Applying the Book's Principles - includes debt payoff planning, strategies for nest egg security, and realistic assessments of the money myths that might be controlling you.

Podcasts:

https://www.daveramsey.com/show/archives

Calculate the amount of debt you owe with the debt calculator:

https://www.daveramsey.com/fpu/debt-calculator

Tony Robbins

You can learn more about Tony's books, seminars, and training by visiting www.tonyrobbins.com.

Books:

MONEY Master the Game: 7 Simple Steps to Financial Freedom - research and interviews with more than 50 top financial experts reveals a universal blueprint with an easy-to-implement sequence.

Awaken the Giant Within - quality improvements to awaken your inherent personal power for maximum satisfaction from a proven coach.

Unshakeable: Your Financial Freedom Playbook - a book of plays designed to accelerate your progress to financial freedom by starting exactly where you are.

Unlimited Power - how to harness your personal mental strength to unlock greater achievements and personal satisfaction.

Podcasts:

https://www.tonyrobbins.com/podcasts/

For more financial insights: Follow the author at
https://www.JayKemmerer.com

https://www.berkshireadvisors.net

BEFORE YOU GO

It was such an honor to spend time with you throughout your reading of this book. I'd like to take just a few more minutes to make a request. It's not a large one.

If you enjoyed this book, would you be so kind as to take a moment, go to Amazon and look up the title *Messages from the MONEY Masters* and/or type in my name: Jay Kemmerer. Once you arrive on my book's sales page, would you please leave a short review? Even if you only had time to go through a couple of chapters you will be able to leave a review and, if you desire, go back later and add to it once you've had a chance to complete the book. Your first impressions are very useful, so don't worry if you only have time now to review one or two chapters.

Finally, note that books succeed by the kind, generous time readers take to leave honest reviews. This is how other readers learn about books that are most beneficial for them to buy. To this end, I thank you in advance for this very kind gesture of appreciation. It means the world to me.

Made in the USA
Monee, IL
16 February 2020